The House on the Hill

Recollections of a Lockmaster's son
growing up on the Rideau

DON WARREN

Trafford rev. 01/21/2025

Trafford PUBLISHING® www.trafford.com

North America & international
toll-free: 844-688-6899 (USA & Canada)
fax: 812 355 4082

INTRODUCTION

EVER SINCE MY eldest daughter, Susan, helped to translate the diary of Peter Sweeney, first Lockmaster of Jones Falls in 1832, I have toyed with the idea of putting in print, what it was like for a lockman's son first and a Lockmaster later, to grow up in those years from 1921 to 1946.

Hopefully, it will fill in the "gap" too often left of the experiences and routine of one boy growing up on the edge of the Rideau at Newboro and Chaffey's Lock.

The names used, in almost all cases, are the real names of those, who in one way or other, played a part in my life.

I sincerely hope that those left out, will not be offended. It was with their help and guidance that all we local kids of the nineteen twenties and thirties moved from childhood to adulthood. The Second World War, of course, was part of our growing up, and played a major role in our lives. Unfortunately, many of us never came back to the Rideau and rest in Europe.

The encouragement I had from my wife, Mary, now deceased, and from my three adult children, Susan, Melinda and David and also my niece Jennifer was outstanding and helped to keep me going.

I would be remiss if I did not mention the great work of Maureen Nolan in helping this amateur put this book together.

DON WARREN

PROLOGUE

I BELIEVE THE Rideau is in my blood because so many of my ancestors had settled first at Chaffey's Mills, prior to 1826 and after the Canal was built, continued to raise their families there.

Some of those ancestors were Sheldon Warren, my great great grandfather and his wife Roby Butler from the Brockville area. His son, Noel and his wife Lydia Whalen, John Warren, my grandfather married Ellen Rowswell, a local girl of English descent, and one of those children was Herman, my father.

The life of the family in the States is very spotty, and hardly necessary for this tale. Let it be known however, that my ancestors were not Loyalists, but were connected in one way or another with the American Revolutionary Army. Those who came to Canada after the revolution were in search of cheap land.

David Bishop Senior, one of the U.S. immigrants, reputedly was a fifer in the Revolutionary Army and his father Gideon, an officer in the same army.

The only one who did not serve in one war or another was my grandfather, Jack.

My mother's family came from near Burridge in North Frontenac. Her father was a retired Belfast policeman named Arthur Thompson, who married one of the Barr family who had come to Canada to work on the locks being built on the Rideau.

I have taken the liberty to write a section called *Guys in Gaters,* a rather rude picture of my own military life during WWII.

The rest consists of some of my poetry, bad or good according to your taste.

I hope you enjoy this journey into the past!

S.S.Loretta. Government Supply Ship. Chaffey's Lock, 1930s

Recollections

I WAS BORN on October 25, 1921 and spent the first two summers of my life in a tent on Newboro lock station.

My dad, Herman Warren had been badly wounded in the face, arm, and hand at the Battle of Cambrai near the end of W.W. I.

Upon returning home, he had married the love of his life, Alice Thompson from near Burridge, Ontario in North Frontenac County.

My mother's mother was a Barr and her father, Arthur Thompson had been a Belfast policeman before he came to Canada after the death of his first wife.

A grateful government of that day, gave wounded veterans first chance to work on The Rideau locks and dad became a lockman at Newboro.

As the lock was too far from their little house, on what is now Bay Street, we were forced to live on the lock itself because it was operated twenty-four hours a day then.

Mr. Dargravel was his first Lockmaster but after two or three years, he retired and "Jack" Lyons took his place. The Lockmaster's house was up the hill from the lock on its north side. It was known as the "Blockhouse".

After our two summers in a tent, Mr. Phillips, Superintendent of the Canal System, gave dad permission to erect a small cabin on a little rise, just south of the upper gates. There is still a flat spot there where the cabin stood.

Alice and Herm Warren at lock in Newboro 1920

Dad had built a picket fence at the front of the cabin to keep me away from the waters. In the fall when the locks closed, we moved back into the village. As we always owned a horse and cow, they too had to be moved at the same time.

When the locks were in operation, I vaguely recollect that First Nation Indians would come through in their canoes and camp for a while on crown lands south east of government property where cottages have, long since, been built.

This memory is reinforced by the fact that one of these nomads gave me a beautiful little hickory bow and six arrows that I eventually brought to Chaffey's Lock when we moved there a few years later. These migrant visitors, were, as a rule, hunters, fishermen and trappers although I believe they also collected "black ash" trees for making baskets.

Other incidents at that time are equally vivid. I remember that my father kept a large pail of minnows attached to the wooden dock right in front of the cottage. One day, probably bored, I decided to escape the picket fence, haul out the pail of minnows, and watch the pretty little fish. To make a long story short, the pail, when I pulled it to the surface, threw me off balance and pulled me into the deep water. Fortunately, dad saw my plight, pulled me out, spanked me, and sent me back to splendid isolation behind the picket fence.

Herm and Alice's Second Home 1924

It did not take me long to realize how dangerous the water could be. This was a good thing to know because as I was growing up it was never more than 150 feet from where we lived.

Another incident I remember was that when mother and I came back one evening from Rathall's store, we found dad, fishing spear in hand, tossing silver eels onto the lock lawn. A large "school" was milling about just above the upper gates. The lawn was literally alive with them slithering about where dad had tossed them. It would appear to me now, that eels in the Upper Rideau must have migrated to the St. Lawrence to spawn, or take a long journey to the ocean for the same purpose. Some were certainly doing this in the late 1920's and 30's at Chaffey's Lock when William Laishley and dad used to operate an eel box off the old plank flume that had carried water to the turbine in the mill at one time. When sufficient numbers of eels had found their way into the box, the men would bag them, take them to the railroad station, and send them to Toronto where, according to local beliefs, "foreigners would eat anything that swam." I think Bill and dad got about two cents a pound for their labour.

At Newboro also, I remember the Ku Klux Clan, an active force in Eastern Ontario in the 1920's. One night they burned a cross near where the new bridge in Newboro now stands. My parents took me up to the Lockmaster's blockhouse and we all watched in awe, (and a little fear) as the white-cloaked figures moved in and out of the light of the burning cross. Many years later, I learned that in the 1930's the "Clan" had died out after a large convention in Smith's Falls attended by some 2000 members. Why they disappeared is still a mystery to me. Years later, however, I learned the names of some of the Clan's members and was surprised to find out who they were. Obviously, the Clan had been used as a vigilante force to frighten citizens who, (according to the standards of the time) were misbehaving. I also remember being with my mother up in the village watching the frantic efforts of a bucket brigade trying to save a building on fire near Landon's Hotel. They were, unfortunately, unsuccessful.

About this period there was a tragic death on the dirt road between Westport and Newboro near where the old cheese factory is now. A local farmer was beaten to death by a tipsy companion. Dad, returning to Newboro from Westport with his horse and buggy came along just after it occurred and notified the authorities, but as far as I know, nothing was ever done to the perpetrator.

That same spring, dad speared a huge pike in McNally's Bay on the Upper Rideau. It was so large, he had to come home and get his horse and buggy to bring it in. Many of our neighbours came to see it. One of the little things that I remember from the Newboro period was my first haircut by a barber. As with many boy babies of the period, I was able to keep my hair long until I was about four years old. (Many boys also wore dress like clothing during their early years). One of my own children, seeing a picture of me in this dress, turned to her mother and said "that's daddy, when he was a little girl".

When I was put in the barber chair and the barber started to cut, I leaped to the floor and headed for home at full speed with my dad at my heels. He returned me to the barbershop and I left later with both ears showing.

About this time, radios were just starting to come into vogue in rural areas, and, of course, we didn't have one. However, one night we were invited by a neighbour who did. He wanted us to come and listen to a fight between I believe Tunney and Dempsey, two of the greats of the period. As I remember, the room was crowded, and as the fight progressed, the men were all up posturing as though they were the contestants – my father included. It was about three years later that I saw a radio again – but at Chaffey's Lock.

My dad, and Fred Randolph, a fishing guide, tried to get a radio set up earlier, but when they attempted to hook up the battery, they blew all the tubes. It wasn't long after that, that dad ransomed his soul to buy a beautiful Stromberg Carlson, which rested on his desk for many years.

I also remember starting to school at Newboro. Miss Henderson was my first teacher and I thought she was the "cat's whiskers". I had just begun to enjoy school when everything changed, because dad was ordered to take over the Lockstation at Chaffey's. Henry Fleming, the current Lockmaster was retiring.

It's easy to remember my father's hesitation, because with minimum education, he was going to take over one of the busiest locks in the system. His inadequacies (or at least believed inadequacies) continued to haunt him until the end of his career in 1957.

Neither dad nor mom wanted to leave Newboro. All their friends such as the Ben Bells, dad's mother and father, and his brother Will who worked in the Spicer cheese box factory were there. It was also a shorter distance by horse and buggy to my mother's married and unmarried sisters scattered about North Frontenac. However, Superintendent Phillips would not take "no" for an answer, and after all, it did mean a promotion and accompanying raise to fifty dollars a month, so the decision was made to go whether we liked it or not.

Life on the Rideau was good in those days. Even though most of the steamers such as the Rideau King and Queen and cheese boats, such as the Rideau Belle no longer plied the waterways, the canal was quickly becoming a fisherman's paradise. Since 1888 when the first locomotive to run between Brockville and Westport, (the engine had been brought to Newboro on a barge), the canal traffic had started to wither. About 1909, when another rail line was being built from Smith's Falls to Napanee crossing the Rideau at Chaffey's Lock, the day of the big boats was coming to an end.

Don and friend. Newboro, 1924

By the 1920's, only canal workboats and the Buena Vista, a coal boat that came from the U.S. to Smith's Falls, survived in this part of the Canal. The Buena Vista had a ferocious whistle, and every time she blew coming around Fingerboard Point west of Newboro, our horse, Prince, would head for the hills. On one occasion when he swam across the canal above Newboro Lock, he ended up in someone's barbed wire fence. He was so badly cut that some thought he should be put down, but, fortunately he lived and was later traded at Tommy Devlin's in Perth for a younger replacement.

It certainly created quite a stir at the time. Mother cried as usual when dad traded or sold an animal, and was teased for it. This time, fortunately, after a good cry, she welcomed his replacement happily.

Newboro was the scene of our first serious family illness – scarlet fever. It would appear that the lock must have been put to bed for the winter because we were in our house on Bay Street. Dr. King, who was eventually to deliver two more of us, quarantined the family for twenty-one days. I can remember the Ben Bells, and dad's brother, Will, leaving groceries on our front steps. A large sign on our door declared to the world that we had an infectious disease and could not go outside except on our own property. As luck would have it, I was the only family victim. When the quarantine ended, I vaguely recollect our house being fumigated with sulphur smoke, which was believed to kill any germs lingering about. Another disease, common at that time, was locally called "galloping consumption". It took its toll on many village young people. If I recall accurately, a young schoolteacher was blamed for introducing it.

In the early spring of 1928, dad moved to Chaffey's Lock where he "boarded" for some time with his uncle Ned Rowswell, who was the lock labourer at the time.

Once when Dad was reminiscing about the "old days", he confided to me how difficult it had been as a young man to have to tell an older close relative to spend more time on his duties and less time rocking on the front porch of his home.

Chaffey's at that time was most likely one of the busiest stations along the whole canal because of the bass fishing so the attention of both operators was needed to do the heavy work of locking them.

At Newboro, mother had to make all the arrangements for our move. In retrospect, we must have been an amusing sight on that day in early May when we set off in a wagon owned by local villager William Spicer with most of our meager belongings in the boxes of two accompanying wagons and with our Jersey cow, Daisy, trailing behind on a halter. Mom, the driver, and a little redheaded bundle that had arrived in the late fall (brought by a "stork" no less) and named Lorraine balanced on mother's legs.

Don Warren, Leon Bell, Charley Bell (L to R), 1928

Our wagon creaked and groaned, the horse broke wind frequently, and mother and Lorraine wept. The two other wagons nestled behind carrying most of our possessions to our new home. I'm afraid I was the only one eager to move for I had missed my dad, strict as he was, and looked forward to our reunion.

My grandparents moved into our empty house in Newboro almost immediately. In those days, there were no "old age" pensions so the children had to shoulder the responsibility for their parent's welfare – otherwise the old folks might be doomed to the "poor house" in Athens. Jack and Ellen (nee Rowswell) lived in our house until they passed away in the mid-thirties.

We travelled to Chaffey's by the Clear Lake road. It was narrow, rutty, and dusty, and in fact, remained that way for years. I remember little else of the trip except that it seemed to go on forever.

About where the busy CNR passed over the road a couple of miles north of the lock, mother spotted a "bob cat" and pointed it out to the driver and me. Those animals had evidently been numerous in the Burridge area near where she had been raised and I think now it made her feel more at home to see one.

When we arrived at the lock, dad (in his official Lockmaster's cap) was there to greet us outside the old stone and clapboard house that we were to occupy for the next twenty-nine years.

It was a long time before St. Lawrence skiffs and kickers became popular at Chaffey's. Nineteen twenty-eight was a banner year for me because it opened doors that had never been opened before. I became a part of Chaffey's and Chaffey's became part of me.

It was late in the afternoon when we arrived, tired and hungry and dad and Uncle Ned helped the wagon drivers move our scruffy furniture into the big stone and clapboard house. Later, we all went to Uncle Ned's place for supper.

Herm Warren and Ned Rowswell at Chaffey's Lock 1929

There were dozens of boats tied up at the locks, many of which were painted with dark green and gold of the Opinicon Hotel. They were mostly skiffs because motor launches were a rarity in those days. The only ones I remember were a large grey launch owned by the Simmons Resort and a large white one owned by the Opinicon. These were used to tow the skiffs and guides out to the fishing grounds in the morning, and return about six o'clock to pick them up.

Two old houseboats were anchored near the locks. One was on a sand shoal at the foot of Boathouse point, and one near the entrance to the by-wash above the lock.

Herm, Lorraine, Don and Alice Warren
in front of the lockmaster's house at Chaffey's 1929

Later, these boats were joined by the "Old Tin Tub" owned by Henry White, one of the colourful guides and the other the Leticia, operated by Richard Mahoney. Somewhat after that, a beautiful cedar strip launch owned, and probably built by George Patterson of Elgin made its appearance. All of these men were important fishing guides of that period.

Perhaps Henry White was the most remarkable of his time. Henry was a real character. He operated a small farm and worked as a fishing guide in the summer. He was fascinated by cars, and had purchased one by the early 1930's. He was also quite eccentric. Rumour had it that when he brought his car to the farm for the first time and was placing it in the haymow, he got excited and shouted "whoa" and went right on out through the back wall of the barn. I remember one time when some of the clients he guided wanted to play a trick on him. Some of them went fishing with Henry, and the others decided to stay home for a rest. Those left at the Opinicon fixed some firecrackers inside the hood of Henry's car and set them up so that when Henry crank started his car, the firecrackers would be set off by sparks hitting the fuse.

As usual, when Henry came in off the lake and was ready to go home, he used the crank, the sparks started the fuses, and the firecrackers started going off under the hood. I came along with the cow just then and there was all kinds of excitement. Henry was shouting "Put the gravel to her, boys", the perpetrators were laughing their heads off and some of the guides were trying to put out the fire by smothering the engine with sand. It was some sight. Even Daisy, the cow, seemed to enjoy it.

He and my father did not get along at all. I remember one late afternoon when Henry and some other guides were coming up through the locks. In those days, heavy weights helped balance the lower sluices and Henry was holding on to the rear gates as the water started to come in. Dad shouted for Henry to move his boat, and Henry shouted back, "You keep to your lock Warren and I'll look after my boat". As the water rose rapidly in the lock, Henry's boat which was below one of the weights got caught, and the boat started to fill with water before Dad and his helper could close the sluices. It was very noisy there for a while, believe me. Incidentally, Henry was probably the only guide who ever saw a sea serpent in Indian Lake and had it chase him down the channel to the lock.

I believe Clint Fleming, a well-known fishing guide, who later in his career authored a book on fishing called *When The Fish are Rising*, was likely one of the first guides to own a "kicker". It was attached to the bow of his skiff, and in my mind's eye, I can see him doing a fine balancing act at the bow so that the boat would not upset when he started the motor. As far as I can determine, Clint Fleming, Dick Mahoney and George Franklin were the forerunners in the sport of "Tree Fishing" for which the Rideau became known. It was during that period that I started to guide tourists – in the early thirties.

The Lockmaster's house was quite a surprise. The house had been built as a defensible fort c1844 but about 1894 a clapboard second story had been added to accommodate the large family of Henry Fleming.

Attached to it on the south west side was a sizeable clapboard kitchen, and on the northeast side, a woodshed. A milk shed was attached to the back of the kitchen.

There was a large two-story barn, which was used for our cow, pigs, horse and hens. It still stands, however, our icehouse, long gone, was just east of the barn and a "two-holer" just behind the barn was our family outhouse. It was certainly a cold run in the winter months.

My mother, Alice was something of a Victorian woman. She seldom visited the outhouse until it was almost dark. One night in July she was sitting there in lonely splendour in the dark when a man pulled the door open and quickly and without seeing her sat down on her lap. I never did hear what went on, but I know mother and the "camper" were both embarrassed by it. In fact, the camper packed his tent and moved out before dawn the next morning.

One other thing sticks out in my memory before the day of modern toilets. Because of the numbers of people camping on the two "points" below the lock, our toilet boxes had a tendency to fill about every two weeks and the stench was pronounced. The big trick was to dispose of this mess in an as out of the way place as soon as possible. A local farmer with his horse and wagon disposed of these containers about every two weeks up where Herman's Road joins the Regan property. His wagon became known as the "honey wagon". He usually appeared about 6:30 PM on the hottest night in the summer. The smell was unbelievable after the driver got the containers on his wagon. On a hot night with a little breeze the smell would drive most of the tourists away from the lock.

No one was upset when at last Parks Canada installed modern washrooms in the woodshed at the north end of the House on the Hill.

The two big elms at the back of the house had a swing, which in motion went back and forth across the road. In those days the road took a sharp turn left in front of the barn towards the Fleming's retirement home.

Ted Ashbaugh and Teddie on lower dock at Chaffey's 1920. Note flume and bridge to mill

Our large garden was on the east side of the road toward the Opinicon Lodge.

The lock itself was much deeper than the one at Newboro, and there was a fast flowing "by-wash" that was used to control the level of the lakes above the lock.

A white grist mill, built c 1873 by John Chaffey was at the lower end to the west of the by-wash, and had a large flume that had carried fast water to the turbine in the lower part of the mill when it was operating. This mill was not in use c1923, although in earlier years many millers had ground grain there. It was at that planked flume that we kids spent many happy hours chasing eels up and down its length and eventually into the "eel trap" previously mentioned, which belonged to my dad and Bill Laishley. Our game was to try to catch the eels by hand. We would corner one, grab it by the head, and often we were left with a handful of slime. Some eels, I'm sure were up to three feet long. Our home on the hill was much larger than the one in Newboro. The living room and dining room were painted dark green, but the kitchen where we spent most of our time in the summer was a dull grey. It still retained vestiges of gun slits on the first floor, however.

All in all, it was a foreboding place for a young impressionable boy, and I feared its ghosts.

My mom, being of Irish descent, had all kinds of scary stories of banshees, knocking on the stove pipes, pictures awry, will-of-the-wisps and birds in the house – all considered to be signs of imminent disaster. Naturally, I believed in them. The darkness of the house, the high ceilings and the unpredictable carbide lights often gave me nights of horror when I was sent upstairs to go to bed alone.

Our kitchen ceiling was plentifully decorated with gouges where one of our predecessors had used a broom handle to waken "Luke", one of their hired help who had slept in a low ceiling room above the kitchen. It could be reached by steps concealed behind a door leading from below. It was a cold place in winter, but in spite of that, it contained a rather decrepit bathtub, which was seldom used.

Mrs. Fleming, "Sarah", had run the Chaffey's Lock post office from the part of the kitchen facing the lock. Of course, when they moved into their elegant new house, she took the post office with her, and it operated from there for many years.

The Three. Musqueteers.

ARTHUR CORDES   Pete Ashbaugh   Don Warren.

After the hunt. Arthur Cordes, Pete Ashbaugh, Don Warren. 1929

Life at Chaffey's in the summer was always lively. Groups of gypsies, we never found out from where, use to arrive at the "four corners", south of Jordan's hill near Elgin on what is now Highway 15. They were a colourful group who use to trade horses with the local farmers, sell trinkets and make their neighbours uneasy. Somewhere, my mother had heard that they sometimes stole white children, especially those with blond hair, such as I was and I remember, in the 1920's when they came to Chaffey's to beg, steal or sell trinkets, she would send me to my bedroom and keep a close eye on those colourfully dressed swarthy women with their tinkling bracelets.

How silly it all seems today, but at that time, it was no laughing matter. As far as I know, these unfortunate wanderers did nothing to warrant their reputations, except perhaps to outwit some local farmers in horse-trading.

By 1930, I was firmly established in the bedroom overlooking the Opinicon Hotel and Opinicon Lake.

Icehouse and chickenhouse. Busty Ashbaugh in front of barn

My brother Doug, was born c1935 in the room at the north corner of the house overlooking the canal. As far as I know, he was the last child to be born in that house.

As a youngster, I knew little of what was happening in the world. We lived in a small isolated time capsule and our only knowledge of what was going on outside our own little space came in *The Toronto Star*, brought religiously from Elgin by Henry Sly, our mailman. It arrived with our mail, wrapped in a round bundle, and was eagerly waited for. Through it, we did learn a little of the Great Depression besetting Canada. The CNR, which ran just west of the village, was very busy with passenger and freight trains, which made regular stops at our station to load and unload goods and passengers, as well as fishermen. Some local students also used the railroad to go to school in Smith's Falls. Because of the Depression, there was little steady work anywhere. Dad and mother felt very lucky to be able to live and work at the lock. Many, men in particular, travelled great distances under horrid conditions to find any kind of employment. They "rode the rails" walked or hitchhiked from one large city to another trying to make a few dollars to send home to their families. These people lived on the road. They were often unwashed and shabby when they stopped at our door looking for a handout. The Lockmaster's house at Chaffey's was like a magnet to them. Many so called "bums" often found themselves at loose ends between Ottawa and Toronto, and without food or money, they were forced to beg in good weather and bad. Our small hamlet had its share of these transients during that time. We felt there was a special mark on the old wooden swing bridge that indicated we were a "soft touch" for these unhappy voyageurs. Now, I just think it was because we were handy and compassionate, that they approached us. In summer it was not necessary for them to seek shelter, but winter was a different matter.

Dad, in spite of mother's fears, would occasionally allow such a person, in the winter, to bunk down on a spare couch for the night in our kitchen. With the fire roaring busily away, it was quite a comfortable spot. However, Dad's generosity did not prevent him from putting a bullet in his old 25 Stevens rifle, and leaning it behind his bed upstairs. He had a good alarm if anything happened, because, I'm sure, mother never slept a wink with a stranger in the house. We never had any real problem with these unfortunate people. I remember one in particular that my father called "Joe" at one time. At one time, Joe had taken up residence in a little lean-to just past the big fill to our west. He use to collect old newspapers and empty bottles from the community. He would then cover the bottles with "paper mache" and sell them as ornaments. He came and went like a ghost, but occasionally he would sit in our kitchen and take full advantage of the heat. He had a foreign accent, and he appeared from nowhere and was going nowhere. As none of us bathed over once a week, often not that, in a large easily moved tub in the kitchen, his odour was not too distinguishable from ours. My father, unlike my mother, enjoyed music immensely. We had an old upright victrola that use to sit in the room nearest the woodshed. There were a large selection of records, and much to mother's disgust, Herm would play them over and over again. Some of them are still emblazoned in my mind. There was "Wait 'til you get them in the air boys – there won't be anyone to watch you there", "The Wreck of the Old '97 – she was going full steam doing ninety miles an hour" – "The Letter Edged in Black", "Please Mr. Conductor, don't put me off the train. The best friend I have in the world sir is waiting for me in vain, "Oh," if I had the wings of an angel, Over these prison walls I would fly, I'd fly to the arms of my poor darling, and there I'd be willing to die" and of course, "Ramona, I'll meet you by the waterfall". This one really got to mother for some reason or other, and I'm sure there was a certain significance to it, but what it was, I never discovered.

When it came time for my brother, Doug, to arrive, mother who had great difficulty in giving birth, contacted Dr. King from Newboro who had delivered both Lorraine and me, and he came with his "horse and rig" to be with her. Lorraine and I were sent off to the new Community Hall with Mother's dear friend Jenny Laishley for a turkey dinner. Jenny kept us away from the house on the hill until the event was over. The new baby, Douglas Bruce, was named in honour of the doctor. The subject of a new family member had never been mentioned to me until two weeks before the big event was to take place. It was then that dad sheepishly mentioned that I was going to have a new sister or brother, brought by that damned stork no less, the one I had never seen. Mind you, I had guessed for some time that something was in the wind.

A young woman from Newboro was hired to help mother for a few weeks after Doug arrived. For the life of me, I can't remember her first name, but it might just be Beryl. I do know, she was away from home in Newboro for the first time. She had been given my room to use while she was with us and I was shifted out into the hall upstairs on a camp cot. Happily, her stay did not last as long as would be expected. The first night there, about 3 AM someone began to scream. Dad dove from the bed, hit his head on the wall and began to swear. Then he raced down the hall where the wild screeches were coming from the girl's room. She was hysterical and shrieked continually until she ran out of steam and began to sob. According to her, between twitches and sobs, a ghost had floated in through the northeast widow over the woodshed, and had hovered over her. She left the next morning for home, and no amount of pleading could bring her back. Mother said the girl had probably eaten too many cucumber sandwiches before she went to bed. However, as I got older, and more worldly and often used that same window to sneak in late, I began to think that one of the Fleming boys down the road at the new house had become confused and had returned to his old bedroom after an evening of festivities.

Winter in the house on the hill 1930s

The carbide lights that were used to light the ground floor of the house were always an annoyance. Also, the open flame, so close to the walls, was considered dangerous.

The gas was generated in a small enclosed area of the woodshed at the north of the house. If the carbide gas was low, the lights would flame up and down throwing long shadows on the inside walls, and dad would be forced to run out and put more carbide in the water to generate more gas. After a couple of years of this frustrating experience, dad, completely exasperated, went out and executed the nuisance with an axe. After that, we went back to a succession of coal oil lamps, Aladdin lamps, and Coleman lamps until hydro arrived in the 1930's to put an end to this inconvenience.

There was also a large galvanized tank on the kitchen roof which during the warm months was kept full of water by a "ram" that was in the by-wash. The tank was heated by the sun and was useful in summer to supplement the hot water tank on the kitchen stove.

A cistern in the basement supplied our washing water in winter. As I recollect, it was drained and dried out every two years and produced some pretty disgusting contents as there were no screens over it.

Our house, of course, was heated with wood that dad cut each fall and early winter in the area west of the lock where there is now heavy cottage development on what we call The Two Doctors. My father did most of the work with an axe and a Swede saw. He was ambidextrous and an excellent woodsman. It was amazing, the number of trees he could "down" in a short time with his axes which were kept razor sharp.

The wood was cut in "sleigh lengths" in the bush for the farmer who would eventually draw it across Indian Lake to the old winter road on the point just west of the railroad and hence to the Lockmaster's house. He did this for fifty cents a load.

As dad worked alone, except on some weekends when I went with him to the woods to pile "brush", the work was dangerous. However, he was very careful and few accidents occurred.

One year, as a boy, he, his father and his brother Will had spent the winter in an isolated "tin roofed shanty" on Indian Lake, not far from where we later cut our wood. After this experience of that winter in the bush, he knew all about the dangers of "felling" trees.

I'm sure dad was often exhausted when he struggled home on the edge of darkness up the long hill south east of the log bridge which was called the Coon Bridge in those days. Not only did he work all day, but walked at least four miles in coming and going.

Rollway of winter wood behind the Lockmaster's House 1930s

When the local farmer brought the wood to the Lockmaster's house, it was piled on the southeast side in a "rollway" ready for the sawyers, who would come in the spring. At that time, Frank Best, once the cheese maker at the Opinicon Lake Cheese Factory at the head of Opinicon Lake, would arrive with his old Model T Ford which was used as a source of power to drive the saw which cut the wood into sixteen inch lengths. One representative from each of our wood burning neighbours would appear, and we would spend the next two days cutting. Although I was young, I was expected to work with the others.

It was dangerous around the saw as it whined and tore its way through the logs when the workers brought them to the "apron". Frank would always make sure they kept the proper sixteen inch length.

Lorraine Warren with wood sawn into 16 ft. lengths

The activity certainly generated lots of tobacco juice and snuff because most of the men chewed one thing or another.

At twelve o'clock sharp, dinner was served. Mother, and one or two local women had been preparing for the "cutting" for a week. The meals were absolutely wonderful with a wide selection of meat, vegetables and above all "out of this world" desserts and hot black tea. This was the only reward that sawyers had, except for the pittance paid to the farmers who drew the wood, and to Frank for his machine.

When our "rollway" was cut, we moved to the next family's and repeated the procedure. Then our wood had to be split before the frost went out of it, piled and dried, and eventually put neatly in the woodshed. We joked that it warmed us at least six times before it was burned.

Occasionally, when the horses drew the wood across the ice on sleights, they would break through. One time in my memory, the Simmons's team broke through, but the horses were saved by choking them. When they were choked, the horses swelled up and floated high enough in the water that they could be pulled out on the ice. To do this, was a very dangerous job because the horses were crazed with fear.

We burned lots of wood at home We had a large stove in the kitchen with an overhead warmer, four holes in the top of the stove, covered with lids, a water heater opposite the firebox and of course, a large oven. It was a very efficient stove, but time consuming to keep burning.

Note the neatness of this woodpile to the left. The rollway is to the right.

My mother, Alice, loved her tea (no coffee for us). Each year we got two large boxes of Daly's Tea from Napanee in large colourful Chinese boxes – one of black tea and one of green. Mother used two spoonfuls of black to one of green in an old aluminum tea pot, which simmered away on the stove every day. If needed, water was added and extra tea. The tea grew stronger as the day passed by and as one could say, "It was strong enough to float a spoon".

Our winter heater was located at the side of the stairs in the living room. Of course, stoves and stove pipes went hand in hand and because the "pipes" gradually became loaded with soot and creosote crystals, they had to be taken down and cleaned each year. A chimney fire could easily result in a house being burned to the ground.

At pipe cleaning time, dad and mom did not work as a team. It was dirty work, often carried out on a warm fall day, and as the pipes had to be knocked out and burned out and then put back together again (no easy job with the pipes of that time), tempers flared all around.

We kids knew enough to keep well out of the way on pipe cleaning day.

Our telephone, as I have previously mentioned, was in the unlighted booth at the west end of the kitchen. Year by year more farmers and residents of Chaffey's were getting phones installed. I believe Henry Fleming the retired Lockmaster was one of the original owners of the telephone company.

As all rings came into each household, (ours was three longs and a short), everyone was able to listen to the conversations.

You could usually figure out if someone was eavesdropping because you would hear clicks on the line and there would be a loss of power. Quite often you could identify who was "eavesdropping" by the bark of a dog, the crying of a child or a conversation taking place in the background.

If the neighbours drained too much power, you could stop for a moment and say, "Fred, will you please hang up so I can hear Jenny" or whatever.

However, the phone could also be used for giving out misinformation as well. All you had to do was suggest that Reta was "expecting" and it would be all over the community the next day.

The phone was particularly of value if there was a house fire. Six rings, repeated over and over again brought us running because there was an emergency somewhere.

I recollect clearly one time when the Darling house at the head of Opinicon Lake caught fire and burned to the ground. We were only able to reach there in time to save a few of the contents.

The barn at the lock, which at this time is still in use as a storage area for Parks Canada, had two stories as well as stalls for our cows and horse. Philip, our horse, use to stay in his stall and on moonlight nights kick the wall behind him. There are still his marks on the wall.

There was also a hidden box beneath the floor of what became our garage, where generations of lock men had kept their booze. As far as I know, it is still there.

Generally our cow, always a Jersey, was called Daisy, and our last horse was called "Phillip" who dad bragged, was a retired "pacer". We also had a chicken run with a dozen pullets and one mean old rooster.

Ordinarily we raised two piglets, which we fattened for winter when fresh meat was hard to get. Mother had a large garden where we grew most of the staples including frivolous items such as sweet corn and gooseberries. The gooseberries made an exceptionally fine jam, and sometimes I was allowed to sell them to summer visitors for ten cents a honey pail.

We ate well. Dinner, our main meal of the day, was always at twelve noon sharp, supper at five and breakfast at about 6:30 AM Dad's temper boiled over if mother was seconds late getting food on the table!

He'd sit at the head of the table with a picture of "The Last Farewell" hanging on the wall at his left, watching the door to the kitchen, and tapping his plate with a fork until mother served the meal. There were times when dad behaved like a tyrant.

Our preoccupation with food was remarkable. Primarily, mother's role was the running of the house and gathering and preparing food.

Our butter and rich Jersey milk came from our cow, Daisy. We had an old barrel churn that could be operated by hand or foot (as I remember) and we youngsters were frequently involved in the operation. We used the rich butter on mother's home made bread, which she baked weekly during the 1920's and 1930's. The Jersey cream was often used on our oatmeal porridge, and we also had buttermilk, which I loved. Mother usually made seven or eight large round loaves of bread a week, and sometimes more in the summer when campers used to stand outside our door drooling. On baking day, you could smell the cooking all around the house, and some days she would break down and produce a few loaves for a little pocket money from the tourists.

Perhaps because it was so long ago, I romanticize mother's bread too much. On the other hand, today's bread, with few exceptions, tastes like cardboard when compared with her big round loaves punched down on the kitchen table and allowed to rise before they were placed in the oven the next morning.

I can almost taste that bread now, warm from the baking and drenched in thick maple syrup from Leggett's farm in Crosby or Charlie Bass's just off the road to Newboro.

A variety of berries and crab apples were gathered throughout the summer season as they ripened. There was a favourite tree on Scott's Island that we use to visit each year because of the quality of the crab apples.

Wild strawberries, some of which were referred to as "sow teats" were the first to ripen in late June. We picked them with enthusiasm because those not immediately eaten in the field were either used as a fresh dessert with sugar and cream or preserved for winter use.

As the wild strawberries were quite small (and delicious, when compared to the tasteless monstrosities grown for sale today) we gathered as many as we could.

Mother and Mrs. Roy Moroughan a friend and wife of the "Lockman" at that time, use to pick berries as we kids did on Saturdays without cheating by eating them. Their berries were normally turned into wonderful jams, preserves, and even the occasional pie.

Later in the season, we gathered "black caps" and wild raspberries (almost extinct in our area in the 2000's) and they too were transformed into jams and preserves, which were stored on shelves in the basement for winter use.

In due time, the "thimble berries" ripened. They were formed like thimbles and were long, black and juicy. Unfortunately, they were grown on brambles that would scratch you badly if you failed to wear long-sleeved shirts and fingerless gloves.

Dad and mother considered them the Queens of the berry world. I can well remember how wonderful they were when made into "thimble berry pie".

Occasionally, in berry picking, we would disturb a hornet's nest and it was "every man for himself" as we hurriedly made out way out of the "patch".

In my last year of elementary school, fall took on a new meaning. The duck season started in late September, and continued until our lakes were icebound.

Dad started taking me hunting with him when traffic on the canal slowed down. How I used to look forward to those Saturday mornings when we visited many lakes in search of Teal, Wood Ducks, Mallards, Whistlers, etc. Dad's favourite spots were on Opinicon, Indian and Benson Lakes, although swamps were splendid for the early departing Teal and Wood Ducks. There were few cottages on the lakes then.

We would leave the house about four AM in the dark – stay for the "morning shoot" (from about six AM to seven thirty AM) and return home in time for dad to begin his day's work.

Herm was an excellent shot, probably because of his WWI experience in France. For the first couple of years, I acted as his retriever (a job which in later years, I had my son, Dave, do for me) to catch any ducks that were wounded and unable to fly, and put them out of their misery. They served as part of our food chain.

When the Wood Ducks and Blue Winged Teal, the first to migrate, were gone, the Mallards and Blacks came in. The big yellow legged Mallards from the north also arrived and, because of their size, were considered a real prize.

Whistlers and Blue Bills succeeded these ducks just before freeze up time and in turn were succeeded by Saw Bills (Mergansers), fish ducks that were headed south. Few geese were coming through in those days. In 2007, there are so many, they have become a nuisance.

All ducks were good to eat except "fish ducks". They had a saying about Mergansers that if you wanted to eat one you put it in a metal pot, added water and red hot stones. After three hours, you should throw away the ducks and eat the stones.

All ducks (except fish ducks) were considered edible. However, there were a few of the guides' wives, particularly Anna Bevans, Tim's wife, who was expert in making a very tasty Merganser stew. I think she must have used a lot of garlic in the pot.

When dad was too busy to take me hunting, Tim Bevans, a most respected guide and story teller, would take pity on me and take me hunting with him. He was an outstanding shot, well versed in wood lore, and taught me a great deal about the nature around us.

In fact, he pointed out one morning, on a pond near Hart Lake, the first fresh water otter I had ever seen. I often watched in awe as he would knock down three or four ducks as they flared over our duck blind.

By the time I was fifteen, I had borrowed an old double barrelled ten gauge shotgun from the Flemings and began to hunt by myself. As my training had been excellent, it was seldom that I returned home empty handed.

By that time I was quite handy with guns because dad had started me with a BB gun when I was about nine years old. During that period I had bagged a number of partridge with it on Wilfred Regan's farm. Mother never considered my time wasted in doing this as she loved eating partridge.

However, this part of my life was not without its errors. I remember one incident in particular when I was standing on a large stump at the lower end of Murphy's Bay and a flock of ducks whipped overhead. In my excitement, I pulled both triggers of the old 10 gauge at the same time and ended up on my back in the shallow swampy water. My shoulder was sore for weeks afterwards.

Birds, as you can see, were an important addition to out fall diet. Unlike our old friend, Jim Simmons, who had a reputation for hanging his dead ducks by their necks in the milk house until their bodies dropped off, evidently an English way of preparing birds for the pot, we ate our ducks when they were fresh. Certainly our family with some three hundred years of North American pioneering did not wait for our meat to get ripe before eating it (unless it was later in the winter).

Before refrigeration became common, many farmers butchered

a steer in the fall just at freeze up time, and hung it in the hay mow where it froze stiff. Then, as they wanted meat, they would saw off a piece for dinner. If there happened to be a quick January thaw, the carcass had to be cut down, and covered with snow to preserve it. Even with these precautions, sometimes, by mid-winter the meat would develop greenish-blue streaks running through it when it was sliced at the table.

Our pigs were also "butchered" in the fall just before freeze-up. We kids got the bladder for a football and that was some recompense for having to listen to the poor creatures squeal when their throats were cut and they were allowed to run loose until they expired. It was always a sad day when the friendly pigs we had fattened over the summer had to be killed, but it was necessary.

When the animals were dead, scraped and cut up, we had delicious fresh pork chops and head cheese.

However, by far, the greatest part of the pig was cut up and "pickled" by placing the pieces in a barrel full of heavy brine kept in the cellar. This guaranteed us good salt pork later in the winter after our gorging on fresh meat had necessarily ended.

It was an important part of our diet, and while at Newboro, quite acceptable, as most people did the same. At Chaffey's however, it was different story. A family by the name of Quackenbush who had been summer guests at the Opinicon for many years, complained of the smell of the pigs nearby, especially when there was a west wind. At last dad was ordered by the Ottawa office to get rid of them.

Potatoes were eaten at least twice a day and sometimes three times. Normally they were boiled for dinner at noon, the biggest meal, and leftovers were fried for supper and next morning's breakfast. Rolled oats were generally part of our breakfast as well. Supper in particular, consisted of leftovers from breakfast and dinner, plus dessert of some kind, generally preserved berries. Occasionally in the summer, we used Daisy's cream to make ice cream – a huge treat.

In our household, salads in season were plentiful. One I particularly remember was made of cabbage and carrots grated and doused with home made mustard and vinegar dressing. We also stored vegetables such as potatoes, beets, carrots, parsnips, and turnips in our basement for winter use.

Maple syrup was on the table for every meal. We all used it regularly with mother's homemade bread. Dad was so fond of it. I swear he use to pour it on his potatoes and meat. However, one summer visitor (a doctor) warned him he would die of diabetes unless he was a little less generous in its use and he regretfully gave it up forever.

Bacon was bought by the "slab", and at times, rolls of smoked ham that would store easily. I saw so much of it as a youngster, I never cared for it afterwards.

In the spring we waited eagerly for the fish to start "running" in the shallows and streams feeding the lakes. Generally, this occurred in the "drowned lands" which were created when the Canal was built between 1826–32.

Our favourite spring sport was to visit the Coon Bridge to the west of the lock, now turned into a causeway in Chamberlain's Bay leading to The Two Doctor's development on Indian Lake.

In the late 20's and early 30's, the pike could easily pass under the floating bridge to spawn. This they did among the cattails and in a creek that drained a beautiful tamarack swamp to the south west.

Big female pike and the smaller more aggressive males would be there shortly after the ice went out.

Needless to say, after the long, cold winter when our regular diet was supplemented now and then by fish caught through the ice, fresh pike fillets were like "manna from heaven". We were all eager to get our share and we did.

However, as time passed and game wardens became common, we became aware of the consequences of spearing, shooting, lassoing, or snagging the fish. The sport then became less and less acceptable, but in no way disappeared.

We kids learned to fillet a pike in the bush, put the fillets in the top of our rubber boots, and return home as fast as we could.

I might add that a good lesson in conservation was learned from this experience. As soon as a new causeway replaced the log bridge, Indian Lake lost one of the best spawning grounds in the area. Not only did the causeway back up the water behind it a foot higher than at lake level, but spawning became impossible, the great tamarack swamp was drowned out, as were most of the Pitcher Plants that had been common inhabitants of the marsh. Some progress!

However, until this occurred, we continued to take fish above the log bridge in any manner, shape, or form we could. This was, of course, because of our ignorance of conservation. The fish were always welcomed at home because by spring, the salt pork left was not nearly as good as it had been in the past fall.

After the pike, the black suckers and red suckers "ran" in the local creeks and the lock "by-wash". Before the logs protecting the upper gates were removed for the summer, pike and suckers sometimes found their was through the lower sluices, and attracted by running water, leaking through the upper sluices, reached a little channel between the logs and the upper gates. Sometimes we would even stand on the upper sill and try to spear suckers as they circled the lock.

Late in April when the wild plums were in bloom, bullheads began to move up into the "drowned lands" to spawn.

Our favourite spot then was well down in Murphy's Bay where it narrows into a bay of wild rice.

On any particular night after April 25, you would find from ten to fifteen trapping boats and skiffs, each containing at least two people, tied nose to tail to stakes shoved into the mud, "bobbing" for bull heads, and telling lies. Later, in the 1950's I believe, The Department of Game and Fisheries made that area into a fish reserve and closed it to all fishing. After a few of the local boys were caught there the next spring and fined heavily by the game warden, it stopped. Soon we moved our stakes to other "bullheading" areas away from the original, but it was never the same.

In those days, it had been easy to catch at least 150 "mud pouts" between 8 PM and midnight. Most people enjoyed eating them and still do in this area.

Dad and I, after a good night "bobbing", would occasionally "skin out" a significant number of fish and sell them to local residents for a few cents a piece.

"Bullheads" ran at night and were dangerous to handle because of the sharp fin on their back and the two, which protruded on the sides of their head. Because the penetration of one of those fins into a human hand had been known to cause blood poisoning, we used the method we called "bobbing" to catch the fish. This made physical contact with them in the dark unnecessary.

A "bob" consisted of thirty to sixty dew worms strung on a heavy black thread with a long needle frequently made from the spoke of a bicycle wheel.

The long string of "night crawlers" this created was then tied together to make a large circle, and then wrapped around one's hand to make a number of smaller rings. Heavy fishing line was then threaded through the rings and tightened until there was a "bob" created about the size of a fist.

The "bob" was then attached to about a five foot length of line which was fastened to the end of a five or six foot dried cedar or white ash pole.

As dark descended, we let our "bobs" down into a clear spot we had raked earlier in the day to get rid of the weeds – one that had even been "baited" with a dead woodchuck. Then we waited for the fun.

The voracious "bullheads" attracted by the ball of worms, would get their teeth stuck on the heavy thread on which the ball of worms had been threaded, and would hang on until lifted, or flung into the boat. It was not at all rare to catch two or three fish at one time this way.

As soon as we felt a bite, we would lift the pole and deposit the fish in the bottom of the boat. We never tried to handle them in the dark.

The making of a "bob" was not pretty. A friend of mine who taught school as I did after the war, not knowing our procedure for making "bobs" actually threw up when he saw what we did.

Occasionally, we would be unlucky enough to have our "bob" attacked by a silver eel. If we boated one, it would go up and down the bottom of the boat throwing slime and water all over us. I remember one night when a friend of mine, Bill Alford, was trying to hit an eel as it slithered up and down in his boat. In the semi dark the snake-like eel on the floor, Bill stood up on a seat and tried to hit it with an oar. He became so upset at the fish that he finally broke a hole in the bottom of his boat, and had to be helped ashore in the dark. His language was inspiring!

Our dew worms were picked by hand at night, but fortunately, with a coal oil lantern, we could collect a hundred or so in two or three hours on the Opinicon or Lock lawns. It was even made easier when flashlights came into use.

The cleaning of the catch took place the following morning in daylight. Dad and I used a leather glove on our left hand to protect us from the bullheads horns, broke the skin at the back of the fishes head, and with a pair of roofing pinchers in our right hand, skinned the bullhead like a banana. Then with the same pinchers, we would cut the backbone at the neck and throw the head away. It was a bloody task.

Another way was used to catch fish in the late fall with nets.

An uncle of mine who lived near Wolfe Lake in the 1930's use to net whitefish in the lake in spite of the fact that it was illegal. Anytime, you could go to my uncle's woodshed after "freeze up" and find a dozen or more big whitefish hanging by their tails from the rafters. These tasty fish were always a welcome addition to a larder.

In the spring, after "bullheading", dad always took a couple of Sundays, after we had a car, to have a picnic and fish pickerel (walleyes) along the dirt road snaking around the south east side of Wolfe Lake.

By then, we had a 1932 Chevy which he would park in a little flat area near the bridge that led to Fermoy, and the whole family, including Mom's best friend, Jenny Laishley, would start to fish.

As I recollect, there was a "bait man" in Fermoy who sold minnows for one or two cents each. There was another family there that grew ginseng under a shed made from discarded pine siding. Some people including a cousin of mine made a living by collecting wild ginseng from the bush.

We seldom caught anything but rock bass in the morning or

afternoon unless a storm came up, but about 5:30 PM, when locals from the village began to appear with their long bamboo poles, "bobbers", and worms or minnows, the "walleye" began to bite and continued to do so until it was too dark for us to see. Obviously, from their large eyes and behavior we should have known they were night feeders, but we didn't.

If the pickerel failed to bite in Wolfe Lake, on our way home we would stop off at Mary Jane's Bridge where Wolfe Lake drains into Sand Lake on its way to the Upper Rideau. We fished there in the current with pretty good results over the years.

Occasionally we would make a trek to Fish Creek, Green Bay off Bob's Lake or Bolingbrook, but particularly to mother's favourite spot she called "Pickerel Rock" not too far south of Bolingbrook where from time to time, pickerel worked their way up to the dam.

Ironically, she always had good luck there – but the rest of us did not. It was also ironic that our mother Alice who did all the honours of cooking the fish, detested them as food. This dislike, as I later found out, was because of a place she had "worked out" as a thirteen year old girl, and was required to go down into a dank cellar every morning and dig around in a barrel of brine for the fish that were being preserved there. Her boss liked them for breakfast.

I reiterate, we ate well even in the worst of economic times (The Great Depression) and most of our food came from the Rideau Watershed. I suppose the sophisticated of today would compare us to tribes who lived by hunting and gathering.

We had a fair sized ice house, a few steps to the east of the barn, which was filled in the depths of winter from ice cut near Berliner's Island on Opinicon Lake, or on the Lock side of Rock Island on Indian Lake. A farmer and his team received a dollar a day to bring the large cakes of ice from the lake to the ice house.

The farmer who drew our ice asked dad every year to leave his meager pay at Halliday's store in Elgin so he could use it to purchase groceries for his very young family.

Cakes of ice were approximately a hundred pounds in weight. Ice house filling and packing the ice house was dangerous. Dick

Mahoney and my Dad usually did the packing inside the ice house where they arranged the blocks in tiers after the cakes had been dropped inside.

The ice house door was located six or seven feet above ground and one or two planks were run from the sleigh to the opening. Dad and Dick would then arrange the hundred-pound cakes that were shoved up from the sleigh to the ice-house door so that there would be a minimum of wasted space. They would then pack between the cakes with snow and added sawdust as an insulator between each layer. This routine was continued until only an escape route was left for the "packers" to get out when the ice house was considered to be satisfactorily full. This ice, towards the end, was almost as high as the roof of the building itself.

In the summer, as we used or sold the ice – at one cent a pound delivered, the process was reversed and it was very dangerous, especially for a youngster. I would have to get the blocks out of the icehouse, wash them, weigh them and deliver them by wheel-barrow to the campers or boaters who wanted them placed in their wooden ice containers buried in the ground. It was the only way we could preserve food in the summer.

As with cutting wood, filling icehouses was a village co-operative exercise that served us well. Little or no money ever changed hands. There were, of course, certain problems associated with ice houses.

The Opinicon Lodge and Simmons's Resort both had large ice houses in which tourists could leave their catches to refrigerate them until time to go home. This created a problem, because after the guides had buried the fish in the sawdust, they were sometimes hard to find, so sportsmen often left them to rot. Cleaning out an icehouse in the late fall was a disgusting exercise at best.

It had its tragic side too. One of the characters who helped fill our icehouses would get so impatient from time to time, that he would place his arms about a cake and throw it up into the icehouse. Physical strength was considered a sign of manhood.

Unfortunately, the physical strain was too great for him and I fear contributed to his early demise. One hot summer when the ice

THE HOUSE ON THE HILL | *Don Warren*

ran out at the Opinicon Hotel, they were said to have found ice in one of the closed mines at the head of Opinicon Lake.

In the summer, we moonlighted a bit and sold vegetables, fresh Jersey milk from old Daisy and, of course, ice to the visitors who were mostly from Ottawa. These visitors arrived about the twenty-fourth of May, erected their tents in prime spots near the lock and went home until the weather warmed up. There was no limit on how long they could occupy the land and no charge as far as I know.

We also served ice to the occasional large vessel passing through and it was a back breaking exercise to get the large cakes on board. Two of my jobs, as I broadened out, were to handle the ice and put out the lights on the channel buoys that marked the safe route to Barrel Point. There were four lanterns, two white and two red, which were, exchanged each evening about five PM They marked the course of the original creek, which had existed before the locks were built. In a motor boat you passed to the right of a red lantern and to the left of a green lantern if heading south. If coming north it was exactly the opposite. This was particularly important because of innumerable stumps that had been left when the water had been raised for the canal. Little remains of those stumps now.

These buoys in those days were small platforms about four feet square fastened to the bottom of the lake with a cement block by chains. Each had a post set in the centre about four feet tall with a wooden arm stretching out to the water's edge. The trick was to attach the handle of the coal oil lantern to the arm and then connect a spring to the base of the lantern to keep it firmly in place in case of a wind. On a windy evening it was very difficult to attach the lanterns. In spite of this, I use to enjoy this part of my work because it gave me a chance to practice my fishing skills every evening from 5:00 PM until dark.

Dad received fifteen dollars a month for this chore during navigation season, as well as all the bass he could eat. In those days it was rare for me to come in without bass. Putting out the lights was a welcome addition to the fifty dollars a month dad got for his duties as Lockmaster during the depression years.

Another of my more embarrassing chores was to get Daisy, our cow, from the field behind the settlers' graveyard about six thirty each morning, and take her back to the pasture as soon as she'd been milked. Dad or mother did the milking – whichever was free. My job was to take Daisy back to pasture as soon as this ritual was completed.

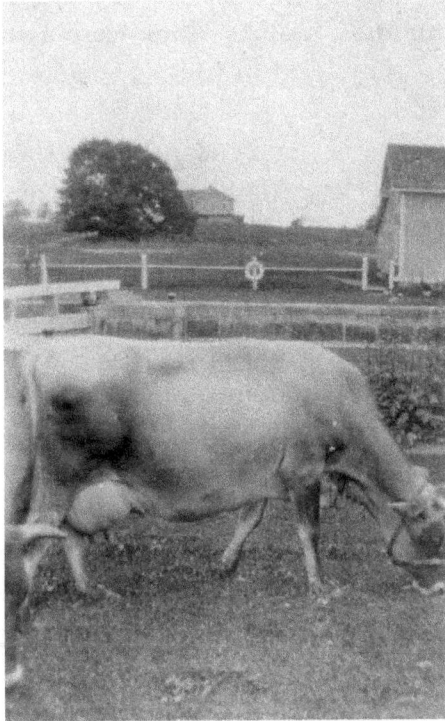

Daisy the cow, the bane of my young life!

At 4:30 PM the cow had to be caught again, haltered and dragged past the tourists who were beginning to come in off the lakes.

Daisy was the plague of my life. Not only would she hide behind the large cedar trees then prevalent in the area, but also she'd balk when I got her near the boathouses. The fishermen thought my problems with the animal were hilarious – but I had to be much older before I could agree with them.

How I envied those Yankee fishermen with their tailored riding breeks, bright checkered shirts and shiny boots. Most of all, I envied

THE HOUSE ON THE HILL

their bamboo fishing rods and their top-notch gear.

It wasn't that I couldn't get all the bass we needed around the lock, but the little jewels of lakes that circled Scott's Island, I could only dream about.

The guides were my "role models" as might be said today. Some thirty-five or forty operated out of Chaffey's at that time from the Opinicon or Simmons's Resorts. They were a stalwart group of gentlemen who, if they lived in today's society, could have been anything they desired.

Outstanding guides, as I remember them in those days were Tim Bevans, Henry White, Henry Smith, Edgar Warren, Bill Doyle, Fred Randolph, Clint Fleming, Dick Mahoney, Bob Lasha, Jack Patterson, George Franklin, Jim Simmons, George Moroughan, Orman Baxter, Ernie Merriman and Robin Fluke. Of course, as with any group, there were occasional renegades who added the required "local colour".

Bass were common in and around the lock in those days. You could almost always spot some at the upper and lower wing-wall. George Taylor, the bait catcher from Newboro, arrived standing up in his motorboat, swarthy complexioned, a peaked cap balanced on his head and buckets of fresh minnows he had caught just at daylight out in his "secret spots".

Cook Rowswell, a local farmer and relative of ours, came regularly with a bag of leopard frogs, used as bait in the new tree fishing craze. They sold for a few cents apiece.

Sometimes, when George headed for home in Newboro, he would leave a large bucket of minnows up toward the Opinicon pump house, and paid Dad a small sum for selling them between lockages. Needless to say, any dead minnows were thrown out, and scooped up by we youngsters who haunted the waters below the by-wash looking for (and often hooking) the big ones. It was not a rare occurrence then to take a 'five-pounder" in the current below the old mill.

A favourite spot for us to sit was on a little bridge that ran just below the mill to Mill Point. Generations of 'lock brats" used these handy spots to help fill the family larder. Unfortunately, the little bridge eventually fell down and was never replaced.

The bay immediately below the lock and down from the Opinicon was true "drowned land" with a variety of water weeds which served as protection for bullfrogs, black water snakes and two or three varieties of turtles such as painted and "big snappers". As a boy, I spent many hours there observing nature, or trying to net large snappers that could be sold to the Opinicon cook for a quarter a piece to make a delicious turtle soup for their guests.

Frog's legs were also considered a summer delicacy, and with our B.B. guns by day, and long poles at night with line and a triple hook wrapped in red flannel, which we dangled in front of the frog by lantern light, we made good money for the time. Sometimes, above the lock in Chamberlain's Bay we could get as many as forty bull frogs in one short afternoon.

These were eagerly snapped up by tenters and sometimes, transient boaters. Too often, the money we made was used to feed the slot machine run by George Jarrett in the Opinicon store. This too was overcome when we found that a cent, when inserted the right way could produce "Jackpots". We nearly drove George crazy.

Every so often a large "snapper" would get caught in the lock, and water snakes would haunt pools in the by-wash looking for sunfish.

One day, Bob Virr, Pete Asbaugh and I found a large fish cage below the Miller's house. We spent the next two or three days collecting about fifteen large and angry black water snakes from the den on Mill Point and placing them in the cage. A couple of days later after we had ignored them too long, they were striking out at anyone brave enough to get near them. Soon, someone complained to my dad, and all hell broke loose.

We were given the unwelcome task of releasing all the enraged snakes, uninjured. Because those snakes had what we called "frog mouths" none of us was injured, but we had some unpleasant bruises on our hands and arms before we worked out a way to handle them.

Nearly every afternoon, when I wasn't busy with chores, I would play tag above and below "the basin" with the campers' kids. Some of us, more daring than others, would periodically run off the lower wing-wall and jump into the "boil" as the water in the lock was released. Sometimes we even swam through the lower sluices when the lock was empty to avoid being caught and made "it" in tag.

As we became older, it became a rite of manhood to jump off the railway bridge, or to spend a night alone during a thunderstorm in the old deserted mill.

Remarkably few who jumped from the bridge were hurt. The water under it was a little deeper than now, and if you threw your feet up when you hit the water, you were OK.

I guess Mick Alford didn't understand this, because when he jumped, he hit the water at a poor angle and injured himself rather badly.

One of my older friends, Bill Acton from Montreal who had strong family ties in South Crosby Township, introduced me to my first bootlegger, "Dollar Bill" in Kingston. Acton had an old model A Ford that took us anywhere we wished to go.

Dances in various villages were like bears to honey for us and we visited many, prior to the war.

"Dollar Bill" was a well known Kingston bootlegger who was set up not far from RMC (Royal Military College) in an old hangar so he had a very select clientele. War was rearing its ugly head in Europe and most young men were "living it" while they could.

Rumour had it that Dollar Bill had been a professor, but I never saw any documents to support this rumour.

However, I do remember vividly that he stated from time to time that if anyone could drink two of his special drinks and walk out, drinks would be on the house. The proprietor talked frequently of the drinks "lacrity of momentum" whatever that was.

Bill Acton had many friends from Montreal who used to visit him at the family cottage near the by-wash bridge.

Garnet Virr, another Chaffey's visitor and a student at Royal Military College in Kingston, use to come down to Chaffey's when he had time off and brought RMC friends with him to Mill Point.

While we younger boys regularly played "tag" about the locks, these older boys invented a special kind of tag for them.

They would take their fishing rods, put "plugs" with three sets of triple hooks on their lines, and play a wild game of tag by trying to hook one of the others and making him "it".

Bill Acton c.1940

I know some of us envied them their beer generated game, but we never got around to trying it.

Most of these young men joined the army shortly and Bill Acton signed on to become a paratrooper in an American-Canadian unit near the beginning of hostilities. Fortunately, he survived as did our friendship.

After Labour Day, all our summer friends went home to various mystical cities in the US and Canada.

In the late 1920's and 30's it was the practice of the time for campers, especially those from Ottawa, to put up their tents on the Point on the May 24th weekend, and to remove them on Labour Day. Some "guides" also put up their tents near the locks so by mid-June, twenty or more tents were in place. Some families I can remember were the Virrs, Cordes, Whitleys, Thomas, Warrens (Edgar), Moraghans, Hallidays, MacIntyres, Asbaughs, and Actons (in a small cabin near the by-wash bridge). The Buskards and Andersons camped above the lock on the north west side.

Other campers came and went, but those referred to spent most of the summer in the country. The Regan family had cottages below the lock on the north west side and the Lisse family spent many summers there. I believe Mr. Lisse was a professor of German at Penn State in the USA. It was rumored that there had been an Indian encampment near Regan's cottages before the locks went in.

Ladies waiting for husbands to arrive from Ottawa 1930s.
Ted Ashbaugh (in bathing suit) was the exception.

Our society in those days was not faultless. A good example of this happened in the 1930's when the "guides", who up to that time had the same rights as rich campers, were forced to move away from the water and set up in an area near the pioneer burying ground. Their new camping area quickly became knows as the "bull-pen". I know my father received orders to make the guides move and that he was deeply troubled. After all, the guides were our friends, and relatives in some cases, as well as area natives.

Obviously, they were unhappy at the edict, but had no choice but to accept the change unwillingly. Fortunately, there was no serious trouble.

I could barely imagine what would happen if such unfair,

discriminatory order came down the line today.

In those days, men working on the canal lived in constant fear of dismissal, and I know that after one of my father's experiences, he never revealed his political preference until he retired in 1957.

People groan about favoritism and nepotism that even today, seems rampant on the Rideau. However, it was much more in the open in the 1920's and 30's than it is c2007.

In our area, and in most, I believe, there were two political families, one an organizer for the Tories, and the other for the Grits.

Chaffey's and South Crosby demonstrated this system well. Mr. James W. Simmons was the local Tory guru, and Mr. Fred Alford, the local Grit guru. This was particularly interesting because Jim Simmons had married Fred Alford's sister and Fred Alford had married Jim Simmons's sister. Both families were distant relatives of my dad because Angelina Warren had married a distant relative, a Simmons when he was the second Lockmaster to serve at Chaffey's.

There were no losers in this set-up because regardless of the party in power at the moment, these two interlocked families carried all the influence. To some degree, they determined where government money for the township would be spent, and who would be hired for government work – particularly important in the Hungry 30's, our depression years.

Dad got a good lesson in this during his early days at Chaffey's when he agreed to take Helen Doyle, a neighbour, out to Elgin to vote in an election. Helen was a Liberal and J.W. was not. Dad had hardly made the agreement with Helen and returned home when the phone rang, and it was Jim Simmons who said, "Herm, if you take that woman out to vote in this election it will cost you your job".

In days of the Great Depression, you didn't risk a good job for family pride.

I know dad had to tell the woman he couldn't take her, and he was ashamed of his humiliation until the day he died, and I might add, he never voted Tory again as long as he lived which was just before he was ninety-eight years of age.

Herm Warren, king (almost) of all he surveys. Old Acton cabin in background

Even later, just after WWII, I remember a foreman of the Rideau carpenter gang was fired on the job by the Superintending Engineer, Mr. A. R. Whittier, for not following the plan for a dock or bridge they were building.

The following day the local Liberal guru from Elgin arrived on the scene and interviewed some of the carpenters. A couple of days later, the Superintendent's decision was overturned, and the dismissed foreman was back on the job. Fortunately for him, he came from a large Liberal family.

In effect, even at the time of writing, there are many inconsistencies in hiring and firing practices.

The Opinicon Hotel had a long association with American owners, and as a result, most of their clientele came from the northern states of the U.S.A.

When we came to Chaffey's, the hotel was owned by Mrs. Mae Phillips, and managed by her son of a first marriage, Don Jarrett, and Hazel, his wife. Don was a gifted artist and during the 1930's produced hundreds of feet of coloured film on life at Chaffey's during the period in which I grew up. His daughter, Janice Cross, has most of them still in her collection although a few have been given to the Chaffey's Lock Museum.

One family in particular that spent every summer at Chaffey's as I mentioned before was the Quakinbush family. They were outstanding fishing people and were guided by George Patterson from Elgin and his two sons Ben and Les.

The Quackinbushes, obviously city people, became very upset by my attempts to develop a loon call. Mrs. Q did not care particularly for my practicing my early morning loon calls from behind the milk shed.

As soon as I became aware of this, I increased the intensity of the calls and even practiced in the evening. This became so annoying to Mrs. Q. that she had an intermediary (one of her guides) promise that she would give me five dollars at the end of the season if I'd quit "my yowling". Five dollars in those days was a fortune, so I readily agreed.

Unfortunately, in the fall, she mistook my cousin, Elmer, for me and gave him the money. I tried to get it away from him, but he was a little older and tougher than I was, and kept it. Life is sometimes unfair.

During the 1930's a regatta was held at Newboro almost every year.

There were many activities on regatta day, but the motor boat races out to the "Fingerboard" and back was a major attraction. Some of the boats were exceedingly fast for their time, and the occasional accident added zest to their part of the regatta.

However, there were also swimming races, underwater swimming events to find out the best underwater swimmers, walking the "greasy pole" to get the flag at the end, and diving contests that brought a number of us to the daylight events.

After dark a "fire dive" where a tower had been erected for

the afternoon diving competition was held toward the end of the evening.

Sometimes "Joney" Whalen, a local person would challenge a soldier from the military camp in Kingston to battle him in the ring. It was always a great attraction because Joney was well known in the Newboro area for his boxing ability, which he had honed while in the First World War.

Large crowds from the various villages nearby attended the festivities during daylight hours, but as darkness descended, some of the campers took off in their boats for their cottages on the nearby islands.

Needless to say, a large number of local boys and girls came from Chaffey's to take part in the fun.

Altogether, it was certainly a well organized and enjoyable event.

In the 1930's, campfires were in vogue. Almost every week on Mill Point there was a communal gathering around a fire where we toasted marshmallows, told ghost stories, and sang. We were much less sophisticated than young people are today.

Later, when we were a little older, we'd start a campfire on a small rocky island on Indian Lake where it could be seen by anxious parents (especially those of the girls) who would make their way to the railway bridge from which they could (or thought they could) see what was going on.

However, we younger kids acted as decoys and stayed on the island with the fire while those a little older would take their blankets and beer and row across to Coon's Point, a few hundred yards to the west.

I suspect they had more fun than we did even though our roasted marshmallows were certainly excellent.

Mary Lou and Miriam Lisse, daughters of the German professor from Penn State, spent a few weeks each summer at Davis cottages. They had beautiful voices and a large selection of camp songs. I vaguely remember a small family tragedy they had when their mother lost her wedding ring on the little sand beach that use to be at the south west end of the concrete monstrosity that stands there today.

As far as I know, it was never found. I believe their descendants still come to this part of the Rideau every summer, especially the descendants of Mary Lou and Mark Horlaker who was a good fishing friend of mine until he passed away not long after the war.

Early in the 1930's the Women's Institute, which was rapidly becoming a strong force in the Community, led the drive to build a hall to celebrate the 100th birthday of the construction of the Rideau Canal. Most of the money was donated or raised by the Institute for the necessary materials, and the volunteer workers were organized and supervised by Fred Alford, a well known local carpenter.

People came from as far as six miles away by horse and wagon to assist in the building. Mel Hughson and his son, George were two of those people. George had an unhappy experience about this time. A horse he was working with kicked him in the head. Dr. Coon was called and met Melvin and George at our house. George had his scalp sewed on without any kind of pain killer.

On May 29, 1932 the hall was ready for business. There was a hand painted picture on the stage curtain donated by Don Jarrett, a couple of coats of varnish on the interior, and bunks on the north side of the little stage for folks bringing their children to various festivities. The toilet was outside and attached to the back of the hall so the stage was roomier than it is now.

A player piano had been donated by someone and added a semblance of elegance to the interior.

The basement contained a furnace and at the time, meals were often served there. The official opening took place, as I recollect, as soon as it was ready for use on the anniversary of the opening of the Rideau Canal in 1832.

Representatives from the Canal were there as well as area members of parliament and local gurus.

We kids from Pine Grove School had recitations and skits, but what I remember most was Virginia Alford, one of Fred Alford's daughters belting out "But Only God Can Make a Tree" until the old wooden bridge across the lock shook and groaned.

J.W. Simmons of Simmons's Lodge was chairman and I remember

his mentioning that my dad was the great, great grandson of Sheldon Warren who had drawn stones by oxen for the locks from north of Elgin in the late 1820's. I know that mother and I were both proud to learn this bit of family history and I was encouraged to find my family's history in the States.

My younger sister Lorraine, then a five year old red head, was growing rapidly and was a real devilskin. She had the red hair and complexion inherited from the Warren side of the family – and I must add, the temper to go with it.

She and Janice Jarrett (Cross) became great friends, and that friendship has continued 'til the present.

My mother had a "green thumb" and grew excellent vegetables, some of which she would occasionally sell for a few cents to summer campers on the Point. I must admit that it was not unknown for some of these campers to help themselves to our garden produce. One example that set us laughing occurred when a single mother with two daughters camping on the Point bought a nickel's worth of lettuce from the garden. As was our practice at the time for such a small item, mother told the lady to go into the garden and pick her own. When the woman returned with a large handful of lettuce to pay mother and searched around for the nickel, the bundle fell apart and six carrots catapulted to the ground at Mom's feet much to her chagrin. I do think mother was more embarrassed than the lady was.

Dad, too, had his experience with "light handed" campers. Normally, he was up about five AM and getting chores done before the guides started locking. This one morning, he heard noises coming from our ice house and the door was open. When he looked out the window, he saw a rather small camper from Montreal attempting to wrestle a large cake of ice out of our ice house door. The bandy legged little fellow looked so funny that dad almost rolled on the floor with laughter as he watched the man struggle to his tent and put the big "cake" into his camp refrigerator – a lined hole in the ground which was covered with an insulated top.

Herm often said later it was worth the price of the block of ice to get to see the little guy give himself a hernia, and even better to know what kind of neighbor we had next door. (Later, he found out that the thief was an important Montreal banker.)

So far, I have avoided dealing with schools as much as possible, but they were the one consistent factor in our young lives.

From September to mid June, we made our way to Pine Grove School, over a mile north of the village, in what else, but a large grove of pines. Fall, winter, spring and early summer we trudged through all kinds of inclement weather. (The roads were much dustier and the hills much higher than they are today, or were our legs shorter?)

I still remember the first day I was sent merrily off to Pine Grove, just down the road – or so I was told. I also remember that by the time I had passed the Doyle home near the foot of a large hill and was half-way to my target when Bill Gifford, who lived in the station house, caught up, tossed me to his shoulders, and carried me the extra half mile to school. He had a brother, Richard and twin sisters Eva and Iva who often came down to the lock. They also use to visit us in the winter to play euchre with dad and mother.

Unfortunately, Bill died while still a young man to everyone's sorrow.

The school was of clapboard with a small front porch facing the road and a big well-filled woodshed at the back. The building, as I recollect, was painted white and trimmed with green and there were two outhouses, one for girls and one for boys – east and west of the school respectively. They were each "two holers" and if the wind was in the wrong direction, very odiferous. Behind the school was a small pond where we played "shinny" in the winter at recess and lunch hour with a tin can and sticks.

The classroom, for there was only one, was big enough to accommodate twenty five or thirty children – from First Class to Fourth. There was a small dais in front where the teachers desk was located and each class was lined up there for instruction at least once a day.

At the back of the classroom was a large stove with a stovepipe oven. When it heated up in the winter, the smell of damp clothing would almost suffocate you. The children's seats were double, and a senior student was usually paired with a junior one. My senior partner was "Mickey" Alford. At every opportunity, he would hit me with his hips, and I'd end up in an embarrassed heap on the floor. Then the teacher would reprimand "Mickey" and all would be safe until he bounced me to the floor again.

Our teacher at that time was Miss Mary Simmons, Jim Simmons daughter, who, when she moved on, was replaced by Miss Helen Gourlay. Helen remained our teacher until I graduated to High School. I believe she was probably responsible for my eventually becoming a teacher.

Both teachers were talented young women who ruled with an iron hand. Both were handy with the old school strap, which was kept in a drawer of the teacher's desk.

God help you if your were a victim. You'd get another walloping when you got home because you had embarrassed your family.

However, I must add that the strap was used reluctantly, only when all else failed. I remember one time Jack Best and I got into trouble for some minor offense and Helen Gourlay made us strap one another in the entrance to the school.

I remember Jack was to strap me first, and he did so with great gusto. When my turn came, I gave him a real working over. However, we still remained good friends for years after.

The school had few books, except for those which had seen many years service. Regular text books and "scribblers" had to be supplied by our parents.

Because of the Great Depression, many of our friends and neighbours scarcely had enough cash to keep body and soul together.

We all lived off the land to some degree, and the land was not always generous.

Some neighbours trapped muskrat in the spring and made a few dollars when a rare "fur buyer" came to Elgin.

During the period there were not many beaver in this area, but skunks were a good price and plentiful. There were times when the odour of skunk pelts curing hung over the road on the way to Pine Grove.

Normally, we carried our lunches to school in old fashioned honey pails. My mother, a wonderful cook, use to make my sandwiches from her baked bread and sent me off every day to school with them. I must confess I often neglected to eat them because I envied the kids who had "store-bought bread" and just left my old homemade stuff in my lunch pail and pitched it over a fence before I returned home.

I'd give my eye teeth to have some of the sandwiches back today, now that store-bought bread tastes like cardboard.

The local School Board, all neighbours, in their wisdom because of the "depression", arranged for foodstuffs to make a hot meal for us at noon in the winter. We had macaroni and tomatoes one day, pork and beans another day, and cocoa from time to time as a treat. Some of our classmates who had little at home, really needed this lunch.

I must admit that I still have trouble with cocoa after all these years. The milk came directly from the cows – there was no such thing as pasteurization, and sometimes, it was still warm from the milking. One day, when it was my turn to make lunch, I found about an inch of sludge in the bottom of the milk pail. The milk had not even been strained. I've seldom been able to look a cup of cocoa in the face since then.

However, the kids who never saw the residue went on slurping it down, happy in their ignorance. "What the eyes don't see, the heart don't breathe"

Our honey pails served not only as lunch boxes, but were often used as weapons on the walk home. I recall clearly the bump on the head I received from Betty Murphy's lunch pail because I had teased her one afternoon about her imaginary boyfriend.

There were many split rail fences along the road and our first attempts at smoking was to find a piece of dry ash rail and light up.

Generally at recess, we were allowed to roam through the pine woods that surrounded the school. We really loved those woods, because in winter they prevented light from getting into the school, so we were frequently dismissed about 2 PM to go home. We couldn't see the blackboard, or even our scribblers for that matter.

At lunch hour we played "Kick the Stick", cowboys and Indians and in the spring, softball, if we could find a ball to play with.

However the whole woods was our playground so it wasn't too bad.

When the pike were running in Rowswell's creek, we made our way along a narrow trail to the little falls east of the school with a pool below it where the pike congregated.

About May 24 every year, we would pack up our lunches and walk to "Woodchuck" school in Clear Lake for our annual softball game. The school was easily two miles away and we walked, ran, and skipped all the way there, supervised of course, by our teacher.

After the game, which was held in a field between the Cheese Factory and the "Woodchuck" school, we struggled home, with some years, a short stop to cool our feet at what later became "Pep" Burt's beach.

That was the one and only "field trip" that was consistent.

One other break in our routine that occurred c1932 was that our annual Christmas party was moved from the school to the new Community Hall in Chaffey's.

Our teacher, Miss Gourlay, spent hours of school time rehearsing various parts or recitations, songs and skits.

I remember vaguely being forced into a duet with a plump, enthusiastic young lady. "Rachel, Rachel, I've been thinking, what a great world this would be if the girls were all transported far beyond the Northern seas."

A successful Christmas party was always a star in the teacher's crown. Teachers were paid anything from $200 to $400 a year, but were highly respected in the community (it that was any consolation to them).

When I was in Senior Fourth, one moonlit night in the heart of winter, the senior classes and teacher arranged for a skating party in the then stumpy bay below the Opinicon Hotel. Helen Gourlay was determined on that particular evening to teach us all to skate in pairs.

When my turn came to skate with her, I accidentally went too close to a stump and she fell and twisted her back. For the next week, she was incapacitated, and since there were no supply teachers to be had, the school was shut down. In spite of the fact that it was an accident, I was considered a local hero at school.

Our teachers taught four to eight classes a day as a rule. Each class was called up to the teacher's desk for instruction and blackboard work while the other students were assigned to seat work. One of the great benefits of a one room school was that each of us who was interested, learned to study alone without constant supervision.

Furthermore, if you had a questioning mind, you could listen to the senior students' lessons or investigate some topic that was of interest to you.

Jack Best, one of our better students, received a gold medal from the province for his excellent work in the Provincial Exams that heralded the end of elementary school. These were held in Elgin Continuation School and were considered very important.

Jack and I were the only two eligible from Pine Grove to take the exam that year, and I received an Honour Certificate. Our marks were good enough so that we were accepted for Elgin Continuation School the next year although Jack chose not to go.

Every spring in public school, around or before the 24th of May, "It's the Queen's birthday, we'll all run away", we brought rakes, baskets and sometimes shovels to clean up our school grounds. It was known as "Arbour Day".

We raked up pine needles, put them in baskets and dumped them in the gully behind the school where we played "shinny" in the winter. As I recollect, some of the girls cleaned their "outhouse, and a couple of senior boys did ours. It was not the most desirable job in the world, but an exceedingly important one.

When the grounds were tidy and clean, we celebrated with a softball game in which only the senior boys and girls took part. Younger students played "Kick the Stick" or "Anti-Eye-Over" around the school. With the sweet smell of spring in the air, it was heavenly.

One thing that made it exciting to go back to school in the fall was that it would soon be time for the annual fall fair in Elgin. We youngsters played a significant role in these fairs.

We grew vegetables to show, raised calves to be judged, did some elementary judging of farm animals and took part in some highly competitive public speaking.

The Fair was generally held close to where Rideau District High School now stands, or in a large field near the road to Phillipsville on the Charland homestead.

As I remember it, there were various levels of public speaking, but generally, the crunch was on the senior elementary students to represent their particular schools.

To be selected to represent your school, you had to go through a "weeding out" process in the school itself.

The teacher frequently selected your topic, and you researched it and developed your own speech.

On a selected day, each candidate gave his talk in front of all the students and was judged.

If you won this initial step, the teacher really worked with you to polish the speech and enhance your presentation.

In my final year, I was selected to represent Pine Grove School and considered it a real honour.

At the fair, when my turn came, I climbed to the top of the wagon box, used as a platform, and gave the onlookers everything I had. My speech, as I recollect, was about horses, and horses were still considered very important animals. To add icing to the cake, much to my surprise, I won, to the great delight of my teacher.

Some seventy-five years later, as I look back, I can see that this was the best training a child could get. What value is it to be bright if you cannot express your ideas to others with clarity?

It is with a great deal of nostalgia that I recollect those days as a canal brat.

When I was almost fourteen, a serious crisis occurred in my life. After a debilitating bout with infantile paralysis, a terrible plague in the area for one winter when it resulted in the death of one student and crippling disabilities for two or three others, I finished public school, and had to prepare myself for leaving my family for the first time.

Fortunately, because of the clear-headed thinking of Doctor Coon and Doctor Norman Kerr , who was training with him in Elgin at the time, my parents were instructed to take me out of school for three months, and make me walk, walk, walk. My parents did this, and it resulted that my left leg, damaged by the polio, strengthened.

A few years later, when I joined the army there was no sign of a limp. It's still hard to realize how far ahead of their time these two remarkable healers were.

Hence it was, that I should go to Elgin Continuation School and board with Cliff and Ella Pennock, Dorothy Perriman (a relative of Cliff's) and numerous ever-changing bank tellers. There were also two girls about my own age, Beulah Mee from Crosby, and Margaret Young from Forfar. These people became my second family during the next four years.

Elgin Continuation School 1935. L to R. Edgar Connell (Toar), Bill Jordan, Don Warren, Allan Baker, Bill Muchmore, Art Baker (front row) L. to R. Dorothy Summers, Anna Donovan, Helen Stone, Eleanor Murphy, Marian Charland, Mattie Stanton, Bessie Haskins, Gertie Myers, Gertrude Doyle

Much later I found out that Cliff, when a young man, had worked at the Opinicon Hotel as a barber and photographer in the early 1900's.

Although he had long since given up photography, he had left a rich picture of life at Chaffey's at the turn of the Century.

These pictures, with the exception of a few local albums, now reside safely in the hands of Parks Canada in Cornwall, or with Don Jarrett's daughter, Janice.

To make a long story short, Cliff and Ella agreed to give me room and board from Monday to Friday at eleven dollars a month. My weekends then, were to be spent at Chaffey's and my week days in Elgin or later at Athens when I was in Grade 13.

The residents there were lively, and though I frequently longed to go home, they made the life of this thirteen year old as easy as possible.

However, I do remember a few problems with Margaret and Beulah who would fix my bed (slats) so that when I jumped into it to go to sleep, all the slats would hit the floor. There would be silence in the barber shop immediately below, and then Cliff would shout, "What's going on up there?" even when he knew very well what had happened.

I have written before of Ella and Cliff for the Chaffey's Lock Area Heritage Society, so I will be a little less wordy here.

They had no children of their own, so they literally adopted all of us.

Cliff cut hair from eight in the morning to eleven o'clock at night. He charged twenty-five cents a head – the going rate then. However, he did not work steadily, so when he wasn't busy, he would often coax me away from my homework to play cribbage with him.

Beside hair cutting and cribbage, he and a neighbour named Pinkerton, use to build fancy cribbage tables made of different kinds of wood. A few of these are still in existence.

Elgin in those days was split down the middle on a religious basis.

There was a Protestant doctor, Dr. Coon, and two Catholic doctors, Dr. Dunn and later Dr. Feeney. There was a Protestant grocery store and a Catholic grocery store respectively. If you were Protestant you went to Halladays, if Catholic to Myers.

Cliff, however was above this rivalry. He treated all equally and

Ella helped him because she never missed a funeral in any church and cried copious tears whether she knew the deceased or not.

So it was, that nearly all families came to get their hair cut at Cliff's, and perhaps spend an hour or so playing cribbage if business was slow. I learned a good deal of tolerance from the Pennocks.

Cliff, just before the war, put on three act farces to raise money for the Red Cross, and many of us who boarded there became participants. As I look back now, I acknowledge this as one influence Cliff had on my later life.

Some Fridays in fall or spring I walked home to Chaffey's after school. In the winter, I skied to Elgin on Sunday afternoons dragging an old toboggan with my clean clothes which mother had washed, and my books. In those days, I was an avid reader of Edgar Rice Burrough's Tarzan books – *Tarzan of the Apes, Tarzan the Terrible, Tarzan and the Golden Lion* and *Tarzan and the Jewels of Opar* are still kicking about my home somewhere. Zane Grey was also a favourite with his western novels such as *Riders of the Purple Sage* etc. I still have a good deal of affection for them.

Books, of course, were hard to come by in those days although my parents always tried to give me books for Christmas.

The route I took to Elgin on my skis was to go down Opinicon Lake, ski across to Barrel Point dragging my toboggan behind me. I'd then cut up to the Davis Lock Road and ski on to Elgin. It normally took about two hours.

If there was a bad winter's storm on Friday night, and the roads were "snowed in", I would struggle down to the railway station near Elgin, wave a checkered flag at an oncoming train, which would always stop and deliver me to Chaffey's station for a quarter.

Sometimes the snow would be so high in Chaffey's that I had to walk along the top of an old rail fence until I got to Whipple's Store near the lock. Then, the road would be relatively good walking across the lock bridges to home on the hill.

I seldom missed a day in High School in Elgin, because my health, after an early start, was remarkably good.

In those days, Chaffey's, like many other summer outposts, could be "snowed in" for a week or more, or until we opened the road with a team of horses and a sleigh. The snow would be so deep, that some of us had to shovel or "break track" so the horses could get through. Somehow, some of the men would find whiskey in Elgin, and would be rather a noisy crowd before we reached home.

We were really isolated during those rare occasions and these isolated outposts were dangerous to be in if your were very ill.

Weekends, if the ice was glare and the moon was out, three or four of us would skate up to the head of Opinicon Lake some four miles south.

The Darling family, four or five about our own age, would have a fire going in a stump near "Telephone Bay" and Sam and John and the girls would be waiting for us. We would all "horse around" for two or three hours before starting the long skate home.

Sometimes in February and March (March being the preferred month) we would go fishing through the ice opposite the old David John Hughson farm. We would skate up from home and there would be teams and sleighs all around the fishing area. At times, even Clint Fleming's old Ford which he used when "running" his nets, would be there as well.

One season, he and his brother "Curley Ned" stayed with us in the Lockmaster's House from Monday to Friday. I remember that period because they went home to Jasper almost every weekend. I also remember that period remarkably well because we seemed to have bullheads for supper every night.

On the other hand, when we fished with the local "gang" we caught bass (some people call them short nosed pike) which now and then they threw back if a game warden was heard to be in the vicinity), northern pike, shiners, (Calico bass) and perch.

I remember most the difficult time we had getting through the ice to the water so we could get our lines down. There were no fancy drills and even a limited number of "spuds" or chisels so most of us relied on the axe. We had to cut a long trench through the ice to reach the water so we could get our lines into it. Generally we fished with short poles of wood with a couple of cross pieces on the handle to wind in our line.

Sometimes when the ice was particularly good; dad would skate to Newboro and buy a few minnows from George Taylor or Elmer Knapp. Live bait was superior to pork rind used by most ice fishermen. The fish caught were well worth dad's effort, but not so attractive to mother.

Every Saturday evening in the summers, the Women's Institute, to which most of our mothers belonged, held square dances in the new hall. These women were, as a rule, teetotalers who could smell a thimble full of booze a mile away. God help any young man (girls, of course, did not drink) who came to the door with beer on his breath. He would firmly and instantly be sent packing by "the keepers of the door", generally Francis Davis, Hazel Jarrett, Jenny Laishley, or my mother, Alice.

From that first time on, the culprit was a marked man, and the "keepers" regarded him with special attention if he ever returned.

It was a simple time. The boys stood and talked at the back of the hall and the girls giggled and chatted in seats along the sides. To ask a girl to dance, you had to run an obstacle course to get near enough to ask her.

Both locals and visitors joined in the festivities. The Coon girls, cottagers at Davis Lock, a large family of blonde-haired beauties, added zest to the scene, as did local girls, and U.S. girls from Mrs. Graves Girls Summer Camp on Clear Lake. Her daughter Meg, use to attend most of the summer doings as well. How we enjoyed those nights as we got older. Ray Rowswell, the caller, would roar out "Orders for a Square", the sets would form up and soon there was a whirling mob on the floor reacting to Ray's "First couple, swing at the head, down the centre and cut off six. Your left foot up and you right foot down. Hurry up folks, or you'll never get around. Everyone swing!"

"Round Dancing" was not very popular in rural areas, but Ted Ashbaugh who came from Youngstown, Ohio, did her best to teach "Pete" and his friends as well.

Now and then, Fred Randolph, one of the guides, and Jenny Laishley would waltz – and they were good at it.

Not only did we young people enjoy the dancing but the hot dogs and cold drinks also.

Every so often, one of the boys would get rambunctious, and a couple of us would quietly escort him down to where Brown's Marina is now located and throw him into the canal. It was a great place to cool him off.

Summer literally flew by in those days, and before we knew it, all our summer pals had departed for home, and we locals were back in Elgin Continuation School.

I made lifelong friends there. The school held somewhere between fifty and sixty students. There were some fine and dedicated teachers trying to civilize the uncivilized. Miss Makim, Ada J Adams, Howard Allison, and sometimes a Miss Dargavel and a Miss Fleming. I deeply appreciate all they did for us, but particularly Miss Dargavel, who opened my eyes to the wonders of Shakespeare. I had been having trouble with *As You Like It* but one day in class it suddenly came to me what she was doing, and I began to enjoy Shakespeare. She had a great deal to do with my deciding to study English at Queens after I returned from the War.

Unfortunately, not all teachers found satisfaction in Elgin. There was little fun for them, and they must have been very lonely. Not only did they have to be moral, but to appear moral as well if they wished to stay around. Local "Schoolboards" in those days could be very vicious from time to time.

By the time I was fourteen, I had spent some days in summer as an apprentice fishing guide and had a few dollars of my own to spend. After that, I improved every summer, and guiding became second nature. I, of course, had loved to fish most of my life 'til then.

The cash I made on top of a "quarter" a week dad gave me, allowed some leeway, and now and then I treated myself with a coke and a chocolate bar from Cliff's Storefront. As the years passed, I began to contribute more cash for my room and board at Cliff's and for the next four years, my room and board was still eleven dollars a month, as it had been when I started high school. I owed a great deal to Cliff and Ella. With no children themselves they treated us royally.

I was a relatively good student at Continuation School, except for French and Latin, which at that time, were considered necessary. When I was in Second Form, my Latin teacher decided I would never qualify in that subject so informed my parents that I should drop it.

As my parents had only elementary school education, and feeling unsure of themselves, they decided to follow the teacher's directions and allowed me to drop that subject.

Imagine my consternation, when years later, I returned from the War and wished to take an honour course in English at Queens, I was informed that one of the requirements would be for me to have three years of Latin. Luckily, with a little worldly experience, I was able to conquer this challenge, and at the same time, found my wife, an ex-Wren who became my partner for the next fifty-eight years. Our courtship was short. After ten dates we tied the knot. How lucky could I get?

Graduation Elgin Continuation School 1939. L to R. Back Row: Alan Baker, Don Warren, Bill Dwyer. Front row. L to R. Gerty Doyle, Dorothy Summers, Helen Stone, Eleanor Murphy, Marian Charland, Gerty Myers, Matty Stanton

I remember meeting Miss Makim at Chaffey's one summer in the early 1950's after I had begun a teaching career. It did me good to see the surprise on her face when I told her of my success with Latin.

By the summer of 1936, I was "guiding" from the Opinicon Hotel. However, I still went out with groups of two or three guides who were older and wiser than I was in dealing with the vagaries of ardent fishermen. In 1937, with dad's help, I had purchased a St. Lawrence skiff with a small one cylinder brass motor called a Kingfisher. A guide who was very ill, needed cash, and sold it to me for sixty dollars (a fair price in the depression years). I named it "Alcibiades" after a Greek who, I thought, was very unpredictable, as was that boat.

With this new equipment, I was able to make three dollars a day – a vast improvement. No longer was I an apprentice guide who did all the dirty work for the more experienced men. I could now take small "parties" out by myself and was no longer responsible for anyone except the people I fished with. How I had come to hate the pot and pan cleanups after lunch with large "parties" Guides in those days had to clean the fish, cook the meal and, when the guests were finished eating, have the leftovers.

I'll admit I had problems from time to time. One that sticks in my mind involved three S.O.S. pads for cleaning out my pots and pans.

While I was preparing to cook one day, I asked a helper to get my coffee pot from my boat and make the coffee. He did, but failed to see the S.O.S. pads in the bottom.

We were complimented on our fine dinner and the clients were particularly loud in their praise of the coffee saying it was the first time in Canada that they had it brewed so well. Unfortunately, no one knew of the S.O.S. pads, even us.

The next morning, our guests could not go fishing because they had to stay near the toilets at the Opinicon. (In those days, I did not drink coffee, so was free from their problems.)

Imagine my consternation next day when I took my coffee pot to the shore to clean it and discovered the remnants of the S.O.S. pads. As far as I know my sick guests never knew what had occurred, and blamed their troubles on the Opinicon food.

Don Warren the fishing guide, 1937

Another day, out with a large party, I was guiding the man who was in charge. As we had a good catch, about eleven o'clock, he wanted me to take him to the dinner place. When he got there, he told me he had a plan to liven things up.

There was a rather thick tree close to the campfire and he had a number of "cherry bombs" that he wanted to attach to the limbs nearest where Fred would be cooking. I concurred and, when I had finished, we attached a long fuse to the fire crackers. My part was to ignite the fuse when Fred Randolph, the older guide was cooking fish, and then go down to the lake.

I had hardly got there when there were a number of loud explosions up near Fred, and in his hurry to get away, he upset the dinner fish into the fire. Dinner was not too successful that time, and the perpetrator was almost thrown in the lake.

One of the later 1930 summers, I decided to take a break from guiding when school was out and found a job with an extra gang on the railroad.

Martin Bowes, my mentor in a boys organization in Elgin, was the foreman responsible for getting the steel changed on the railway lines on curves from Elgin to Sydenham.

School friends "Toar" Connell and Edmund Kenney were also employed as well as some thirty others. As we were in the throes of the Great Depression, it was not hard to get cheap help.

The first day taught me that it was the toughest job I had ever tackled. We went to work on a "jigger" at 7 AM and returned home about 6 PM We received the noble sum of thirty-three cents an hour for this torture and worked at least ten hours a day.

Because I was fairly large, I was paired on the tongs with Gerry Steadman, a local giant of a man who was also a well known "guide" on the lakes. Twelve of us, six at one end and six at the other end of the rail, use to lift them and turn them around so that the worn side of the rail was now on the outside. Jerry, of course, was so much taller and heavier than I was, had to bend his knees and his back. People who lift heavy objects will tell you that if your knees and back are bent, you are not carrying your share of the load. For about three weeks, I felt as though I was carrying the whole load – which, of course, was double weight.

The heat in the "cuts" was ungodly, and from time to time fights broke out among the workers.

One in particular that sticks in my mind was when one worker started making jokes about another man's girlfriend. He was attacked with a sledge hammer, but managed to outrun his assailant. Martin who had observed the conflict, sent them both away on the first train that came through, and we never saw them again.

I also recollect how my hands blistered because I had forgotten my work gloves one morning, and remember how painful my hands became.

Ed Connell, a lifelong friend, occasionally spent a night with us in the Lockmaster's House on the Hill. Mother always welcomed him. I also remember how angry my dad was because I was making more money than he was.

As time went on, the return to "guiding" became better and better looking every day. Don Jarrett and Jim Simmons needed guides, and wanted me back. Thus the decision was easy. I went back to the lakes, a sadder but wiser teenager.

In 1938 I was eligible for an official Guides License, which I wore proudly on my fishing hat, and as my skills increased, so did the number of clients who wanted an active time on the water, rather than just dragging a minnow behind the boat! It, too, had its drawbacks, because in tree fishing, the guide was forced to spend too much time climbing trees to free hooks caught on the limbs by "greenhorns".

In the fall, I felt rich, paid a good deal of my expenses at Pennocks, helped dad pay a few dollars on an insurance policy he had taken out for me, and managed to buy a second-hand bicycle from Fred Fleming whose father was at the time Captain of the S.S. Loretta, the supply boat then on duty in the Canal.

Compared with most kids my age, I was rich.

Just in case the reader might think that all was "milk and honey" for the guides, let me put them straight.

Traditional guide's dinner

Some of the older "guides" were amazing people. Ed Curry, who lived in Westport, use to go through Newboro Lock about five AM He would then, row to Chaffey's, some five miles away, guide all day with a client from the Opinicon Hotel, and row back to Westport at about seven o'clock at night. He was also a barber and would cut hair until about eleven, and would be on the move the next morning, to repeat the day before. If there were no clients for him when he got to Chaffey's he would lock through and pick blueberries in a patch on Hart Lake. Ed was quite a man.

You had to be very diplomatic to be a guide. I remember one morning taking a father and son up to Hart Lake. I took a skiff behind the motor boat so we could portage about a quarter of a mile uphill to reach the inland lake. When I let my clients out of Alciabiades, and pulled the skiff up on shore, I heard the father say to the son "Lets walk up to the lake, and Don can bring the boat and tackle"

Guide Don at lower end of Hart Lake Portage, 1946

There were a few tense minutes, and then I made it perfectly clear that I could not go over the portage without help. We certainly didn't get to Hart Lake that day.

Another time, going into Hart Lake with a couple of healthy male clients, I got caught again – but more seriously.

Our problem that day was much more serious. When we got over the portage, I shoved the boat out in the water, and one of my hefty gentlemen jumped in. Because it was a rocky shore, and the skiff was on a rock, my clients weight put a hole through the bottom and water started shooting in.

We managed to get the skiff out, turn it over and observe the problem. Because the men were both capable of swimming, and were good clients, I decided to try to fix the hole and then go fishing.

Fortunately, I always had a good knife, so I found a birch tree, cut about a ten inch square of bark, went down to the motor boat and got some heavy grease which I placed over the hole, and with some thumb tacks, managed to make the boat seaworthy. We had a great day fishing.

Guide and client. A big one that didn't get away. 1938

When I took the skiff back to the lady who had rented it to me, she insisted I get a boat builder to repair the hole. It cost me twelve dollars, the equivalent of four days work.

When you were a youngster, you usually got the "party" that was a one day wonder.

I don't know why Don Jarrett sent me out with two important politicians. One, I believe, was Canada's representative in Mexico. He was an arrogant SOB who continued to bully me when we got to our fishing area at the head of Opinicon Lake. The "bass season" hadn't opened yet, and after a couple of hours we had two pike, and suddenly the guest of the Ambassador caught a large bass.

Don and Alcibiades 1939

As it was getting near lunch time, the Ambassador told me to go ashore at a nearby "dinner place". When I went to throw the bass back, he reprimanded me, and said we would eat it for dinner. He was furious when I put the bass back in the water, and watched it swim off.

In the afternoon, he decided to get me, and insisted I take them to the centre of the lake and row fast while they trolled.

I can tell you, there was no tip for me that day, and not only that, I lost a great deal of respect for our, so called, representatives.

One day, I remember on one occasion, when I had to hold a drunken client in my boat to keep him from jumping overboard. He was very abusive.

Then too, there were the sentimental parties who drank too much in the morning.

One of my clients, a favourite, became maudlin after a number of beers, and staggered to her feet every time my little inboard passed an island. She would then wave wildly at the island and shout "Goodbye little island and God Bless." I guess he must have heard her because she reached the dock at the Opinicon Lodge without falling overboard.

If fishing was poor for her, and good for her husband, she would take a swipe at him with her old steel rod. He took it in good humour, thank heavens. I also believe he was some forty years her senior.

There was lots of fun and games then, but it would take a book in itself to repeat them all.

However, when my father retired from the Canal, he decided to try guiding, and all went along fine for a few years.

Then one year, he got a client from the States who was really fond of him. Unfortunately, when on holiday, this client was a real tippler.

One day, coming home across Indian Lake, he shouted at dad over the noise of the motor that he was going to jump overboard. Dad said, "Go ahead, you damned fool" and the client did. Dad, who was in his late seventies at that time, tried his best to get the man into the boat, but when he couldn't, he lassoed the man under the arms, started his motor and towed the client to shore. It was a wonder the fisherman wasn't drowned, but he continued to fish with dad for the next four years when he came to the Opinicon.

On the other hand, there were really excellent people such as Paul Howard and Ed Moulton, both connected to Marshall Field and Company in the States.

I fished with them, on and off for four or five years after the war. After one or two weeks, when we had fished day and sometimes night, they would ask me to figure out my bill and then gave me exactly twice what my bill was. These were representative of many of the excellent people we had the pleasure to fish with.

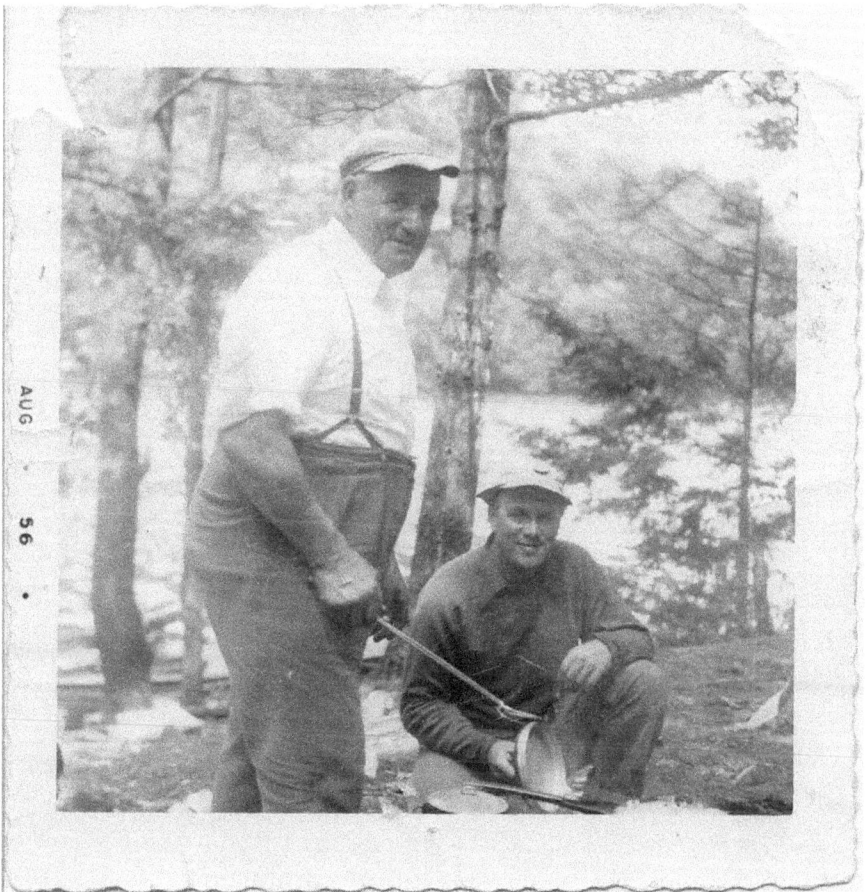

Shore dinner, 1939. Jack Patterson and Don Warren

My income took some pressure off dad and mother at home because they had to begin thinking about an education for my sister Lorraine, who had dreams of becoming a nurse, and my brother Doug, fourteen years my junior whose future also had to be considered.

Dad and mother might as well have raised three families because there were seven years between each of us.

I was proud and felt independent because no longer was I a burden on the family.

A happy client relaxing after lunch 1939

School life went on and it wasn't half bad. The teachers were dedicated and knowledgeable, and most of us there were eager to learn because it was a privilege to be able to go to school in those days.

We took English, Latin, French, Science, Mathematics, History and Civics, which was the study of local government.

Each year as we advanced, the courses became harder and harder, until, at the end of your fourth year in Continuation School, if you had graduated, and if your could afford it, you had to go to Athens High School for your Fifth form. You needed the last year if you had any dreams of University, but University was still the stomping ground of the wealthy as, unfortunately, it is becoming in 2007.

Fishing guides and client's son
(L to R) Russell Franklin, Client's son, Don Warren, Bob Lasha 1946

In the meantime, at Elgin Continuation School, we worked hard and played hard as well. There were plenty of sports to keep us busy. For amusement, we could go bobsledding at night on Dunn's hill in the village, or on Jordan's hill, just west of the Catholic Church on what is now Highway Fifteen. With my home-made bob-sled, I could sometimes reach the four corners at the bottom of Jordan's Hill – no mean feat in that day. God help anyone dumb enough to attempt it today because of the constant flow of traffic both going and coming.

We could skate on a pond near Kenney's on the north west side of Elgin, or some years, on the rink that was eventually built behind E.C.S. where the senior's apartments are today.

Howard Allison, our only male teacher, when not baby-sitting his large brood, would teach us tennis on the north side of the school, and in September and October, we boys played a rough form of football in the field to the west.

I remember Mr. Allison best, because of a near accident that could have burned down the school. One day in the Chemistry lab, he put a sheet of paper with a small chunk of phosphorous on it on my desk and left it to go to another part of the room. When it caught fire, and the students were ready to leave the room to its fate, Howard came and extinguished it quickly.

At one time at Elgin Continuation School, we even had a Ping-Pong table and the competition for school champion was fierce. Ed Connell and I met head to head in one confrontation for the championship – Ed probably thinks still that he won it, but I can assure you, he did not.

We also had a "field day" in the spring or fall, organized and run by our teachers for both boys and girls. There were foot races, high jumps, hop-skip-and-jumps, shot put and pole vaulting. Most students participated in something.

In my last year at Elgin, I managed to get the all-round championship. This was more than likely because I had set up a jumping area in our garden at Chaffey's and had practiced there every weekend.

For the good of our souls, we had *Tuxis Boys* in the Elgin United Church Hall. I still remember that "Tuxis" stood for "Training for service, with Christ in the centre and you and I on either side with no one but Christ between us."

Martin Bowes, the railway foreman who was our mentor, believed in toughening us up, and as well as offering food for the soul, Martin believed we should be able to take care of ourselves, and hence, introduced boxing as well as spiritual things. This was a heroic step on his part because churches were not often used for this rough behaviour.

Bill Muchmore, whose ancestor was one of the early lockmen at Chaffey's, and I, would whale on one another without mercy until Martin would tell us to stop. Unfortunately, Bill was killed in wwii.

Besides introducing me to religion (my family was part of the heathen Warren branch) Martin taught us to be capable of looking after our own interests when challenged, and to remain cool under pressure. With war rearing its ugly head, these qualities were good to have.

He taught us to be God fearing, and helped us to overcome some of the aggressiveness all young men experience just before manhood sets in. By teaching us to "put on the gloves", we later owed him a great deal for his foresight.

Another close friend of mine, Alan Baker, the bank manager's son, was technically inclined and deeply interested in building a crystal radio set.

We would work together by the hour in the attic of his house putting all the pieces together (or we thought it was). We would make an aerial and move it about trying to pick up one of the few stations then broadcasting.

I have no recollection of our every getting a sound, though sometimes I went as far as holding the end of the aerial between my teeth.

However, this fruitless enterprise did kill many hours after school. Later Al's ambition led him to become the owner of Versafood and eventually a millionaire. He also had a lovely sister who became my first serious girlfriend.

Television, at that time, although in its infancy, was just on the edge of becoming a reality, but in Elgin, we were unaware of this.

Two major events occurred in the winter of 1937–38.

One was a terrible ice storm during a school week that would equal the ice storm of 1998. The trees soon became loaded with ice and the sound of breaking branches was really frightening.

At least two inches of ice covered the streets and the roads, and some of us skated as far as Phillipsville, others as far as Delta and, of course, watchful parents were out in full force.

The daughter of a local gentleman, who kept a close eye on her even in the best of times, had disappeared. Her father skated up and down the streets in an effort to find her and even went as far as Phillipsville. However, she eventually turned up, and just where she'd been during her dad's search was a lively topic of gossip for a number of days afterward. One young man in Elgin knew how to keep his mouth shut and the gossip eventually disappeared.

It was a different world with different moral standards in the 1930's. Nice girls were not supposed to smoke, drink alcoholic beverages, or associate with boys who did. According to today's standards, we were a really puritanical group of young people.

Another event that stands out in my mind was a skating expedition with Clair Walker, the teller at the Bank of Montreal, who boarded at Pennocks and was a strong rival for the attention of Dorothy Perriman, who did women's hair. Later they married before Clair went overseas.

One Saturday afternoon after the ice was clear, Clair came to Chaffey's to go for a skate with me.

I had decided to take him around Scott's Island starting at the Benson Creek end. I guess I did this to show off my knowledge of the Rideau. I also knew that the ice in the smaller creeks would be strong because not much water was flowing through the Chaffey's Lock by-wash and that the only questionable places would be at Bedore's Creek, the Elbow between Clear and Newboro Lake and the Isthmus between Clear and Indian Lakes.

It was a beautiful afternoon with little wind, and what there was, would generally be at our backs.

So it was that about 3:30 PM we started merrily on our way through lower Benson, Mosquito Lake and through Bedore's Creek, which joined what was then called "Little Mud" by the guides.

By the time we got there it was beginning to get dark and with no leaves on the trees, the shoreline of Scott's Island could have been on another planet after we had passed Stout's Upper Bay.

I did sense, however, that the Elbow was not far off, and that to pass through it in the darkness that was setting in quickly, would be a disaster. Not only that, but the Elbow was noted for the current that generally kept the water open there.

Hard as I peered into the increasing dusk, I couldn't spot a landmark to tell me just where we were.

Another fifteen minutes slow skate toward the north and I spotted some lights in Crosby in the distance at the far end of what we then called "The Bog", so at least I knew our position.

The next challenge was to find the Carrying Place between Newboro Lake and Clear. It was impossible for us to find now in the darkness so at last we decided to climb over the rocky ridge that separated the two lakes. If you every tried to climb over a rocky spine on skates in the dark, you will know how challenging it is.

Fortunately, we made it without incident, and were soon on Clear Lake where I knew the treacherous Isthmus between Clear and Indian would be.

It took only a few minutes to cross Clear Lake and to reach the home of the Etherington's caretakers. Of course, I called home at once to assure my parents that we were OK. Mother, who answered the phone, was more than a little annoyed. Dad had just gathered together a small group of neighbours and they had started across Indian Lake trying by lantern light to follow our skate marks. They were all quite sure that we had gone to an icy grave.

We at once left the comfort of our neighbours house and went down to the lake shore of Indian Lake where we could see the rescue lanterns snaking up towards Benson Point.

Was there great joy when we appeared out of the darkness alive and well? I had never seen dad as angry as he was that night and never did again. I doubt the Clair ever forgot it either. He never went skating on the lakes with me again.

Clair is no longer with us. He married Dorothy Perriman, went overseas in WWII, and settled in Gananoque where he eventually became mayor.

I graduated from Elgin Continuation School with good marks, and my parents, proud of my success, felt that I should go to Athens for Grade 13.

Even today, I can still remember parts of the Athens High School song;

> *"Cheer for old Athens*
> *Athens must win*
> *Fight to the finish*
> *Never give in*
> *You do your best boys*
> *Will do the rest boys… etc."*

It was also determined that I would continue to stay at Cliff Pennocks in Elgin, and would travel each day to Athens in one of Allie Patterson's seven-passenger cars. Allie also ran the telephone exchange in our village at that time.

He was just starting a bus company, which would grow amazingly in the next twenty years and would move children to various schools in the area.

This, I believe, was his first venture and he received twenty-five cents a day for each passenger he transferred from Elgin to Athens and back.

Ordinarily, I recollect, he carried thirteen students in each of two vehicles. We were piled into each of his cars, and boys and girls together made it lots of fun.

Allie was a remarkable character. He could "blow his top" one second and be perfectly reasonable the next. We all liked him.

He was, however, very excitable, and in the winter when roads were bad, he could be hard to get along with. One winter morning in the middle of a raging snow storm, Allie insisted on starting with his students to Athens in spite of the fact that the road was just about impassable. There weren't the great snow ploughs of today to keep the roads open. We had reached the old tin school house between Elgin and Phillipsville when we hit a big snowdrift and went crossways on the road.

Allie insisted that all we boys clamber outside and attempt to get him out of his predicament. With such a great chance to miss school, we shoved him farther into the ditch. I often wonder why he didn't have a stroke. However, his language was so hot that it melted the snow all the way to Athens.

I believe when we got there, the school was closed. Allie melted some more snow and we returned to Elgin for a half day holiday.

Poetry was quite popular in those days toward the end of the 1930's. I remember how the girls use to blush when we teased them in verse about their imagined escapades.

Athens was very different from Elgin Continuation School. The principal, A.J. Milhousan, was a bright man, somewhat past his prime, but a great father figure. He wanted me to become a dentist, which I knew was impossible, because my parents, with two other children to educate, could not afford to send me to University.

By 1939 we were hearing all kinds of frightening noises from Germany. The sounds emanating from Hitler's mass meetings was unbelievable. It was quite possible that Principal Milhousan was well aware that before long, many of us would be in uniform.

The day war broke out, I was in Allie's car on the way to school when someone casually brought up the subject. I don't think any of us thought, that in the next year or two, we would be on our way overseas.

At A.H.S. we were full of devilment. As the weeks slid by, we were becoming more aware of the danger Hitler posed for the whole world and that boys who had already graduated were "signing up".

I had made a number of good friends at the school, especially Lindsey Smith and "Soup" Yates, both outstanding in their own way.

Lindsay, the son of a minister, was a daredevil. I guess he had to prove that he wasn't a saint although his dad might have been one. He had an agile mind and could think of all kinds of devilment to get into.

The first time I became aware of his dare-devil tendencies was at lunch hour one day when the principal was absent. Lindsey found his way to the roof of the school and entertained us by walking on the little ridge of bricks by holding onto the edge of the roof.

I later learned of his experience on the school bus when he put a firecracker into his lunch pail on the way home, lit the fuse and sneaked up and put it behind the driver. Of course, there had been a loud report, the bus driver almost ditched the vehicle, and Lindsey was put off. As the story went, Lindsey grabbed a bumper, and was finally tossed off when the bus went around a corner. Rumour had it that his shoulder had been badly injured.

Another time, trying to attract the attention of some girls at an old quarry swimming hole on the way to Brockville he, upon being told of the poison ivy nearby, said he was immune to it and rubbed it all over his body. Unfortunately, he was not immune, and as the

85

tale went, he ended up in the hospital again.

He and I were the only two students taking Chemistry with Principal Milhousan as our teacher. He use to set us with tasks in the lab and then read his morning paper, so naturally, we felt free to do as we wanted. Lindsey, spurred on by the war with Germany in sight, decided we should try to make some gun powder, and I agreed.

Eventually, we confiscated a soap container from the boys' washroom. It looked like a little bomb and could be screwed apart to put in soft soap. It also had a little nipple through which the soap came out.

We emptied out the soap, cleaned the inside and filled it with our homemade gunpowder. Lindsey set it off below the hill behind the school by setting a match to a hand made fuse and tossing the "bomb" into the air. Fortunately, the explosion did not wound any of the spectators, but it did rattle a few windows in the school. One part also buried itself in the soft ground right near Lindsey. He was indeed lucky he wasn't killed or injured.

We were never brought to task for it, as I remember, because those who knew about it didn't "squeal".

A couple of years later it didn't shock me to hear that, as rumour had it, Lindsey, in training for the Air force tried to fly under a bridge that was too narrow for the plane's wings and was killed. His own family were the only people who really knew what had happened. Rumour in those days ran rampant.

We had some remarkable teachers at Athens, such as Jessie Wilson. Jessie taught history classes in a very peculiar manner. She use to make us memorize two pages of history every night as homework. I know that I shuddered every time I was told to stand and recite, but fortunately, I always enjoyed history well taught or not.

Jessie's uniform was a blue skirt, a red sweater and black horn-rimmed glasses. She was frequently criticized by the girls in the hall because of her attire. She was a shy person, whose odd approach to history fascinated me. I think she influenced me to take History as a minor subject at Queens after the war.

We were out of school early in June that year so we could help on the farms. Examinations were canceled, and if your earlier marks had been satisfactory you received a pass. I know that I passed French only because of this.

I also remember Brenda Sheridan from Soperton who use to be picked up by our bus. She and Al Baker became great friends for a while.

During that period, as I recollect, Church of England students, on holy days, could get excused from school to go to church.

It was amazing how many of us became instant Anglicans.

That summer is still like a dream. I knew that my major interest was boats and a second, flying.

When I went to Ottawa to "sign up", a summer friend from Ottawa, Douglas McIntyre, who was older than I was, took me there.

I decided to try the Navy first. When Doug let me off at the Naval Recruiting Centre no one appeared to see us by ten-thirty. At last a stout fellow in a sailor's uniform appeared in our waiting room to tell us that the staff members were having a tea break. When nothing occurred in the next half hour, I got out of there as fast as I could It is remarkable the little things that change your life.

I was disillusioned by the Navy, but not enough to restrain me from marrying an ex WREN – some seven years later and staying with her for the next fifty-nine years.

However, having written off the Navy as inefficient and overly British, I told Doug that I thought I'd join the Air Force and become a fighter pilot. He tried to deter me by telling me that the Air Force was very "picky" right then. I was in such good shape, I didn't pay any attention to him, and ended up in the Air Force recruiting centre where all was organized and working as a well oiled machine. After all, I had Grade 13 from high school, and that was considered a good education in those days.

I passed the physical with flying colours until I came to the eye test. To my sorrow, I found out that I did not have strong enough eyes to qualify as a fighter pilot at that time. They told me to go home and wait, and if eye requirements became less demanding, they would be in touch.

It was ironical that when in 1943 I was long settled in a Canadian Wireless Section in England, my C.O. got a request from the Air Force to transfer me to them so I could be trained as a fighter pilot. Obviously, eye requirements were not longer at the top of their lists.

However, because I was fascinated by the nature of my work in wireless intelligence, and was becoming a "Y" operator, I asked to stay with my unit and my commanding officer backed me completely.

Before I was accepted for training by the army, I had worked in Anderson Brothers store in Kingston, then on the corner of Princess and Division Streets. I had done this expecting to be called by the Air Force at any time.

As I believed I should prepare myself for army life, I signed up with the P.W.O.R. a Kingston Militia unit laughingly know as "P. Willies on the Run".

I did, however, get some worthwhile practice twice a week in the City Armories.

When I was twenty, and had not heard from the Air Force, I returned to Ottawa, went to an Army recruiting centre, and three hours later volunteered for wherever they wished to send me. They even asked me what organization I wished to be placed in and I said the Royal Canadian Corps of Signals, partially because Vimy, The Wireless Training Centre, was only about forty miles from my beloved Chaffey's Lock.

After a period of basic training in Cornwall with guns, route marches, parades, bayonet practice, etc. I was sent to Vimy.

Basic Training in Cornwall had been tough. We marched miles in full gear, lived in huts that held too many people, learned about rifles and machine guns of the time, and in general, got to know what was expected from us.

I was about twenty when I got there and with my twenty-first birthday in sight, I planned on going home for a week-end. Unfortunately, some sloppy soldier had left his dirty underwear on his bunk in the morning and so our "leaves" were canceled and we were confined to barracks.

Many of us were very upset at this turn of events and a good number decided to take "a leave" regardless of the results.

Some of us sneaked down to the railway station and I caught a train taking me to Brockville where my dad was to pick me up.

After a great forty-eight hours at the House on the Hill, I returned to Cornwall and was immediately arrested and deposited in the camp jail where a number of my unit were also deposited.

We spent the next three days in the "digger" doing all kinds of dirty work and were all fined four days pay. That first night, a member of our group was almost caught while smoking in his cell, but had dropped his lighted "fag" through a hole in his cell wall. Unfortunately, it started a fire. He is probably still in that jail.

It was shortly after this that I caught mumps (from a cat in the barracks, I believe) so was quarantined for twenty one days in a medical hut with two francophones, who although they knew English, refused to speak it. There was also an officer at the other end of the hut being "sweat out" for alcoholism.

I spent twenty-one days in this hut with no conversation except from the medical people who visited from time to time. It was, beyond doubt, one of the most trying times I had had to date while in the Army.

As soon as I was back on my feet, I was sent to Vimy and my training as a line and wireless operator began. It was great to be treated as a human being again, and to be able to get an occasional chance to go home to my beloved Chaffey's Lock.

At Vimy I became deeply involved in studying Morse Code and other methods of signaling. For the next two or three weeks, I was afraid of being tossed out, but about that time, I passed a test on receiving Morse Code without error at thirteen words a minute. This assured me a place in wireless and in my particular case, reaching the thirteen words a minute, was a plateau. Before too long I was reading Morse at twenty five wpm. Later, in England when I could read at thirty wpm without most errors, I was one selected for a new unit called *Three Canadian Wireless Section, Type A,* that was being formed.

By mid winter and with my initial training completed, I was ready for overseas. After a short leave with my family when my father wept because he knew what I was facing, but my mother suffered wordlessly, I returned to Vimy. One day shortly afterwards our "draft" was told to pack, was given a steak dinner in the mess, and about ten o'clock at night a troop train was waiting (in a miserable snow storm) for us just outside Fort Frontenac. About one PM we were on our way into the unknown.

I was ordered to stand between two of the railway cars when going through Montreal to see that no one tried to disembark there. My rifle and bayonet at the ready, I stood nervously in place. I guess my prayer had been answered because no one jumped from the area that I was responsible for.

There were few comforts on the troop train. The air inside the cars was blue with cigarette smoke, and the odour of stale booze and damp uniforms. Card games were in progress and it was noisy – a little hell in itself.

As I recall, we half dozed on our board seats at least those of us not in a partying mood.

We stopped the next day at a French town and did a sort of route march to clear our heads. Our next real stop, as I recollect it, was in Halifax, where *the Queen Elizabeth*, probably the largest ship of the time, was waiting for us to go aboard.

Rumour had it that some sixteen thousand of us would be on board, and that no protective warships would accompany us.

Evidently, the "Queen" was powerful and speedy enough that enemy submarines could not catch her. We also learned we would be aboard for at least five days. Nine of my buddies and I were on board and settled into our tiny room long before the "Queen" started her zigzag course for England.

Evidently, at some time during our crossing, the enemy declared that we had been sunk, however, that was not the case. Canada was soon out of our sight and we began our journey from tropical to frigid as the "Queen" took her safest course. It was well known event then that every so often, the enemy claimed to have sunk her. I t would be a long time before those of us on board would be fortunate to see her again and of course, many didn't.

My dad's unit going overseas in WWI had some verses that applied to us as well. They went something like this;

Goodbye Canada, we're away to fight the foe

We're sailing tomorrow over the deep blue sea

And we don't know where we're going

But we're on our way

For I belong to Johnny Canuck

And I'm proud to say

That I'll do my do-oty night or day

We don't know where we're going

But we're on our way

England here we come!

Guides at Chaffey's Lock to 1940

Harold Austin	Orman Baxter	Tim Bevans
Louis Burtch	Ed Curry	John Dorey
Bill Doyle	John Fleming	Ned Fleming
Thea Fleming **	George Franklin	Russell Franklin
Robin Fluke	Delbert Hutchings	Berton Halladay
Emily Hughson*	Bob LaSha	Gordon McCready
Jack Murphy	Johnny Murray	Ernie Merriman
Richard Mahoney	George Moroughan	George Patterson
Les Patterson	Ben Patterson	Johnny Pendicook
Fred Randolph	Tom Simmons	Jim Simmons
Ted Simmons	Henry Smith	Johnny Watters
Edgar Warren	Elmer Warren	Don Warren
Henry White		

In the 1920's and 30's these were the guides of Chaffey's (as far as I can remember). They were followed after the war by some of the same guides, as well as a number of new members, – some of whom, still "ply the trade".

* Emily Hughson was the first woman guide at Chaffey's in the 1920s

**Thea Fleming, the second female guide in the 1940's Clint Fleming's daughter.

These were the only females I know who took tourists fishing.

This poem was written by Captain "Ned" Fleming (1868–1953), one of the last steamboat captains of the Rideau, and a descendent of Chaffey's first Lockmaster.

During his long career, he was captain of the Rideau Queen and Rideau King, which operated between Kingston & Ottawa – running night and day.

Captain "Ned" frequently put his thoughts into verse – in this case, inspired by Lake Opinicon at night.

THE GHOSTS OF THE OPINICON

Come with me and I will show you, a gem of the Rideau chain
If a fairer lake you look for, you may well look in vain.
Fairy isles rise from the waters, and silently form a sight
Whose beauty fills the human heart with wonder and delight.

The wooded slopes, the green isles, the waters sparkling sheen,
In beauty shine today, as they did in days pristine.
On its shores wild potatoes grew in days long past and gone
The Indians ate them, liked them, and called the lake "Opinicon".

At night o'er the quiet lake hangs an air of mystery
'Tis said that at the midnight hour, people often see
A little boat out on the lake, that doth swiftly and silently glide
Without-paddle or oar to propel it, o'er the mistly moonlit tide.

At times three people in the boat, sometimes, only one,
The one they say is the ghost of Thomas Dennison.
He was drowned as he towed a raft, in sight of his own door
And 'tis said that he labours still to bring the raft ashore.

Perhaps he is joined by Joe Leway, who died in a mine near by.
Under a rockfall he lay for hours, and no one heard his cry
Now at night his voice is heard, in tones of agony
"Help, help, save my life, please lift this rock from me."

The third one may be Samuel Poole, who drew his latest breath
On the lake shore, where the frost king, closed his eyes in death.
He went to Kingston, to get the pay, for lumber he had sawn.
Next day he was seen to leave, for his home on Opinicon.

From that day for many years, his fate was quite unknown.
Some people thought, with the money, to other land he'd flown.
But after forty years had swiftly come and gone
Children one day found his bones, on the shore of the Opinicon.

It is thought that on that day, from Kingston he had come
Full forty miles, where now he was but three miles from his home.
An icy wind blew down the lake, a blizzard from the west.
He went ashore at a sheltered spot, for a few minutes of rest

Something seemed to tell him, "Don't stop here. Go on."
But he brushed the snow from an old log and with a sigh sat down.
He thought, for ten minutes only, here he should remain
While he gathered strength to face that bitter wind again.

Ah, the blessed feeling of rest, there in that sheltered place
As with benumbed hand, he rubbed his frosted face.
Nodding he fell asleep, only ten minutes rest he was taking
Alas, it was the sleep of death, that knows no earthly waking.

There was a light in the window of his cozy little home
Where anxious hearts were waiting, for one who would never come.
His loved ones searched far and near, and time flowed swiftly on;
But they never knew that his bones lay on the shore of Opinicon.

Joe Leway's spirit lingers, at the mine, 'tis said
Where 'neath a rock for hours he lay, with none to give him aid.
And now each night with a crowbar, he rolls the rock aside,
And goes forth to join other spirits on Opinicon's silvery tide.

The body of Tom Dennison by man has never been found,
Until the lake gives up his bones to lie 'neath a flowery mound,
He will struggle with the raft, to gain the wished for goal,
Tho' at midnight, he may cross the lake with Leway and with Poole.

At times, 'tis said that Dennison. goes wandering forth alone,
Or he may have with him, Leway, who died beneath the stone.
Sam Poole may sometimes join them, and then, this ghostly three
Will glide o'er the Opinicon, swiftly and silently.

For never the creak of oarlock or sound of paddle dip,
Not a word is spoken, by any ghostly lip
Until the hour of midnight, then breaks the magic spell,
And they talk of things of long ago, on the lake they know so well.

All long dead, their spirits linger yet
To wander o'er at the midnight hour, the lake they can't forget.
Reminders of a long forgotten day, why should they linger here?
Like dead leaves drifting quietly from a long forgotten year.

And all their ghostly whisperings, at midnight you may hear,
Though you may never see them, the little boat their spirits steer
You may hear their quiet voices, speaking in varied tone
If at midnight you would listen, to the Ghosts of Opinicon.

Guys In Gaiters

IT ALL STARTED when I was twenty. I packed my little bag, bid fond adieu to my sorrowing parents and took up the sword for King and Country.

Gosh I was a hero! Everyone in my hamlet shook my hand and wished me luck and told me all about the heroic sacrifice I was making. My hat wouldn't fit for a week afterwards – so I went to Ottawa.

It was a hot breathless morning when I finally found myself standing before a smiling officer.

"So you want to join the Army, do you? Well, that's fine – we wish there were more like you – name, address, religion, married or single? Thank you, no, go right over there to the fellow with three stripes and he'll tell you what to do next."

Egad – miles of men, men with pants, men without pants, hairy torsos, smooth torsos, whiskers, no whiskers – dozens of them.

"Now, open your mouth – say aaaahhh!

How do you feel? Any serious ailments? That's fine. Sarg, send this man to Bank Street for an x-ray."

More walking – beautiful C.W.A.C. at x-ray machine – click – "Come back in the afternoon."

Come back this afternoon – Quite!

Four days later I awakened in front of a fat man with three little do-dads on his shoulder. "Now, raise your right hand and swear after me "I, D.H.W., do hereby swear."

I was in, nothing outside of Hell or High Water could get me out.

It was only the beginning.

Another lineup – off with the old, on with the new. "What size pants? Don't know, eh? Give this Joe a pair of eights and one of tens. After a twenty mile march he'll be lucky if he can get into two twelves.

Heavens – what had I got myself into? Webbing, yards of straps – long straps, medium straps, short straps. Big pack, small pack, water bottle, toad stabber, gaiters, shorts, puttees, uniforms khaki.

I was buried in the stuff.

"Corporal, show this man how to get dressed." So that's what these fellows are with one stripe on their arm – attendants. Did everyone have one? I wondered.

An hour later, I stood up and admired myself in all my glory. It sure wasn't any *Esquire* who attended that first parade, but I didn't mind. There were lots more like me.

New soldier at Ottawa 1940 – Ouch!

First inspection. "Sergeant, doesn't this man know how to wear gaiters? You've got them on the wrong legs, boy!"

"See that this man gets a haircut, Sergeant!

"He's supposed to be a soldier – not another Veronica Lake."

"Stand at attention when you are on parade."

"Say 'Yes, Sir' when you're spoken to – wipe that smile off your face – you're the only thing worth laughing at here.

Parade, stand at ease! Attenshun! Dismissed."

Never were more welcome words spoken.

I pulled up my pants, set my wedgie at a rakish angle, put my hands in my pockets and ambled across the drill square towards the barracks.

"Take you hands out of your pockets! Pick up your feet! You may not be a soldier yet, but I'll damn soon make you one."

Thus my first encounter with the C.S.M. Nice bloke! Another week slid by – Quite the soldier now, military brush cut, straight gaiters, magnificent stride, ram rod bearing. Pretty soon they'll make me a 'lance jock' or even a Sergeant, I thought. Wrong again!

It happened this way.

Don Warren, old soldier on the straits of Dover, 1942. What a change!

In the course of the first hectic days, I'd struck up an acquaintance with an old soldier – a tried veteran of at least a month. Little did I suspect the blight this friendship was to place on my first touch of army life.

His name was Hilliard, and he was a nice kid. French, short and very energetic. In a few days we were close friends, sharing all my cigarettes and his company.

Now Hilliard knew about a hole in the fence where we could sneak out after hours. Most soldiers know about one sometime in their careers, but Masson's was special.

To reach it, it was necessary to crawl through a thorny little hedge, wait until the sentry changed, and race like blazes for the barracks.

One particularly dark night, Hil and I were creeping through the hedge as usual, when an extra long thorn made its way into my britches. As I cursed, trying to extract it, the guard appeared.

"Halt! Advance and be recognized."

The irony of it all. Seven days C.B. – Dishes, piles of dishes, mountains of dishes, pots, blackened pots, greasy pots – work, work, work.

It did teach me a lesson though. A little self-control can save a heck of a lot of sorrow.

All hope for rapid promotion gone, I applied for a weekend pass.

"So your sister's having a baby? Why must you be there? Her husband's overseas, you say? Well O.K. – Just this once, mind you."

Little did he know that my only sister was still in the pig-tail stage, but what he didn't know couldn't hurt me.

Home at last – Mother's hero – good home cooking. The old man proud as a peacock and the kids tumbling over themselves with enthusiasm. The girl friend wearing that special look in her eye, and that glorious sense of freedom.

Wonderful! It was then I first actually appreciated the army – at least, that time one actually spent on leave.

Monday morning back at six –

"And how was the baby? Twins?? Good, Excellent. You're on draft."

"Where?"

"Sorry, can't say yet – military secret, regulation 1766493, you know. Get packed! You leave for Cornwall at 1300 hours."

"1300 hours – just what is that in civvy time?"

"One o'clock." "Oh, I'd often wondered."

Fate, however, intervened on my behalf and I found myself at one o'clock reclining in a little white cot surrounded by Medical Officers galore.

"What happened? What did you eat? Didn't you want to go to Cornwall?" etc. etc.

"No, Sir, it was the food at dinner that caused it. It was awful, sir."

Shocked looking officer – M.O. to questioner "I must insist that you leave this soldier alone. He's suffering from ptomaine poisoning."

Shocked silence from the Lieutenant, then, "You don't say so! I'll look into it immediately."

Sirens – fifteen of us to hospital, quiet at last. You know, food poisoning isn't so bad after all.

Five days rest, five days leave fishing, swimming, hunting. God bless all army cooks.

Back to the Ottawa Bull Pen and on draft for Cornwall.

Full marching order, two kit bags, staggered march to the station with six hundred other guys. Long bare train, hard leather seats – chug, chug, chug and away we go.

Fine farmlands of Ontario rolling past. One hour stop – "Everybody out! Line up in threes! Quick march!"

New camp, high barb-wired fences, huge parade ground with the sun glaring on it – long tarpaper shacks, shiny boots, blancoed web – pressed trousers. Basic Training!

Little did I know what I was getting into – little did I know that such pleasant surroundings could cover up such a hellish sweatshop.

"Pick up your feet! Throw back those shoulders! Swing those arms! Hey youse guys what in hell you tink dis, a picnic party?

Stand at attenshun – man in the third rank, pick up your dressing! Correct that slope! Left, right, left, right, forward march."

"Peg that man. Teach him to button his pockets for parade. Double up there. Can't spend all day waiting for you to pick your nose."

OBSTACLE COURSE

"AND NOW FOR a nice change – the obstacle course. You'll get it twice daily from now on."

In my time at Basic, I saw more casualties inflicted on that torturous racetrack than I did in my first year in a theater of war.

Another 48 hours at home.

More starlight in those lustrous eyes!

Back to camp – stiff neck. "You've got the mumps. Twenty one days for you in isolation. Collect your kit!"

So it went on, week after week. True, our cheeks bronzed over, our bearing was better, we ate like horses, but there was resentment – resentment deeply founded in the fact that while we swore, sweltered and sweat, anyone with pre-war knowledge of hockey went swiftly ahead in the ranks escaping the endless drudgery of the common soldier.

We realized we were going to fight a war, but our fat well fed officers – the so called backbone of our army, were more interested in playing around with a two-bit hockey team tying up many good men who were badly needed overseas, than they were in seeing that fair play was observed and that each man played his part. Oh, "the know it all" attitude of the officer corp.

Basic training did go on, however, slow, tedious, back-breaking work.

"And now the obstacle course; you'll get it twice daily."

If you have never endured this particular torture, let me explain it to you.

The ordinary obstacle course was placed in a rough strip of ground approximately a third of a mile long.

Within the borders of this strip of land, our N.C.O.'s attempted to turn us into a mixture of Supermen and Flash Gordons. There was every sort of trap imaginable in ours, and we ran it in full battle order, often after a ten mile route march – a remarkable feat for the strongest of men and a physical impossibility for the average that previously had earned his living from the depths of a padded leather chair.

First, there were two long parallel frames from which a ladder was slung horizontal to the ground and high enough that a man with his arms at full length dangled two feet above the ground.

You were expected to go hand after hand across, and if you slipped, or weren't in condition and fell, you were forced to go back and try it over again.

Next, there was a long track of old tires through which you must run by placing your feet in each tire.

After these came a series of high board fences, a couple of long over-water jumps, a race across a slippery log with a watery trench waiting to receive you if your slipped, and a series of swings over filthy pits of stinking mud ... in my time at "basic".

"Oui, non, c'est bon, n'est ce pas?"

Huge, ungainly jowls, male orderlies, gruel, hospital blues, dinky red tie – "O.K.. You're clear." Five days at home, sick leave – Hell, mumps ain't so bad, after all.

Wonderful time, good fishing, bright October sunshine –

Back to camp, twenty mile route march. "Where are those size 10 boots?

Christ! Will it never end?

Then on Friday afternoon, the inevitable question. "Can I have a 48 hour, sir?"

"Definitely not! You're C.B. to camp."

Can the army do this to me? No bloody way! Show a little initiative Warren. Home sweet home – I'll take it anyway. They can't shoot me for that, can they?

Camp again, lovely night – my birthday. Twenty one glorious years behind me.

Marched to the guard house, a little smelly room – ten other guys, some of them familiar. Gee, is that all they do to you?

Up before the major. "Take off that hat! Right wheel! Quick march! Halt! Left turn!"

"Your name? Aha, AWOL from 1400 Friday till 0001 Monday. Hmm – take him back to the guard house!"

Up before the colonel – "Left wheel! Quick march! Take off the GD hat! Right Wheel! Halt! Left turn!" "Aha, – Any excuse? Will you take my punishment?"

Did I have an alternative? No, of course not. Slight consideration – very slight – "Yes sir!"

"Good! 96 hours detention – loss of eight days pay – take him away!"

Bars on the doors, bars on the windows, bars all over the place and not a drop to drink – little thin blanket, "can" in the corner for whatever – no nuthin.

Furtive puffs from a stub, slight smell of smoke in the air.

Roar! "Whose smoking?"

Guards all over the place – cigarette rolled in stocking – smell of burning cloth –

"Oho, so it's you!"

"Put him in solitary, bread and water – That'll teach him a lesson."

24 dismal hours, no one to talk to, dark, damp, no bed, but a board –

Crime sure doesn't pay in this outfit!

Good wholesome punishment – Nuts!

Four days later, a very crumpled and subdued soldier emerged from the barbed wire enclosure and ambled sheepishly to his billet. It was me. "Never again," I told myself, and I meant it at the time.

More long lines of men, another parting troop train – off to advanced training, bless the Lord.

Somber voice in the background, "Just wait 'til you hit Advanced Training; you'll think Basic was a cinch" – Nuts again!

Suave 90 Day wonder: "So, you want to be a signals operator do you? Why?"

Timid reply: "Well, sir, I understand they're non-combatants and I don't want to be killed."

"Non-combatant! Balls – "Any experience?"

"No, sir!"

"Do you understand Morse code?"

"Do you mean Joe Morse, sir? I think he was with me in Basic Training."

"No, no, Warren, International Morse Code."

"No, sir!"

"Well, Warren it doesn't seem likely they'll accept you, but you'll get a fair chance. Now go to Room 47B and you'll get a test."

"Yes, sir."

Strange ungodly whistles from earphones.

"Are these two sounds alike? Now these, and these, and these?"

Pause – "You didn't get one right. Wait! Don't run away. We need operators so I'll give you a break. Sergeant Brown, Fix this man up!"

Happy, happy days! Operating company, here I come.

Long noisy code rooms – "Now, all together, dit dah, Ack; dah dit dit dit. Beer, Louder please!"

Day after day, week after week. They drilled us. Our backsides broadened, our shoulders rounded, our brains went on hold.

"How fast can you read, Yip?"

"About 4 words per minute."

"Just 4 wpm? Well, I've only been here five weeks and I'm reading six."

"Goody, Goody for you, Sucker."

Forty miles from home – every week-end off – special midnight pass, movies, dances, feminine companionship.

Wonder how my love lights holding out – hope she doesn't hear about Mary. She just might not understand. Women seem funny that way.

More long dit dashing hours.

"Doin' ten words a minute, eh Joe? Pretty soon you'll be goin' overseas."

"Nothin doing, Chum. I'm stickin' to 10 wpm for two months yet. I may be red blooded, but I have no inclination whatever to show it."

This Advanced Training is a cinch – nice clean bunks, nice clean work, no fatigues, Hell, why didn't I come here in the first place?

Good bunch of guys here too. All speak English. A first generation Pole sleeps across from me – names Wojtanowicz or something like that – likes to drink a lot – says it relieves the heebie-jeebies. Beefs like heck when he gets up in the morning – Hates P.T. before breakfast.

Yip to P.T. corporal: "Hey, Corp, how about forgettin' the jerks this morning?"

Corporal: "Rise and shine Wojtanowicz!"

Yip: "No use gettin' up, I ain't doing em nohow."

Corporal: "You won't, eh? Disobeying a direct order. That's a serious offense in this man's army. How I'll give you one more chance, Get up!"

Surly silence from Yip.

Corporal: "O.K. son, you asked for it. Appear at the Orderly Room at 1400 hrs. Is that straight?"

Yip: "Yup!"

Fourteen hundred hours – Yip under close arrest between two tall guards marching to the guardhouse. Night in the cooler – Dismissed.

Yip: "Heck fellas that wasn't so bad. Better than doing P.T. any day."

Cold icy mornings, frozen noses on drill square, out at 4 AM in our B.V.D.s.

Officer: "Now boys, this is only a fire drill, but next time it may be the real thing."

Profanity in all official languages.

"Fat bastards up in the Ford building didn't come out, I'll betcha – what a democracy!"

"Cripes, what minds some of those brass arsed heroes have – don't get enough to do so they think up fool tricks like that."

Back to bed, up at seven. Army life is no bed of roses, believe me.

Shortly after seven o'clock every morning, the long noisy code room – poor ventilation – small fat C.W.A.C. flirting with the Sarge. Its one way of getting good marks for sure. Wish I had a dress and low slung shock absorbers – one way to get places in the army. Then I could pass too.

Another 48 hr. pass. Gosh they're good to us. Must be a catch in it somewhere. The army always has an ulterior motive, believe me!

I rushed to the telephone and after two hours in queue while some Johnny ironed out a quarrel with his lady love, I heard the sweet voice of my mom.

"We're snowed in down here, but if you can hitch-hike as far as Elgin, we'll have a horse and cutter there to meet you."

Hitch hike 40 miles? Fifteen below zero! Aha, sweet youth, what ambitions? What endurance? What damn foolishness?

Walk, walk, walk, now I'm doing it on my own time.

Another car rattled by.

Fat, selfish civilian. Doesn't appreciate what we're doing for him. Just sits back and whistles as though he didn't see me. I'd sure like to get my hands on his beefy neck.

"Whoops, goin' my way mister? Good, I'm stationed at Vimy, Yes, yes, I like the army (like heck!) So you're a veteran of the 1914–18 do? So was my dad; machine gunner with the P.P.C.L.I."

Oh, you were an artillery man, eh? Good outfit! Bet you had a tough time."

Seven miles of snow – snow piled up in miniature mountains – bitter cold wind – half obliterated sled track. Even nature seems to deal us deuces.

Home at last – half frozen, gradually defrosting, hot supper with Mom's famous bread. There's nothing like home. The Joe that wrote "Home Sweet Home" sure had the right idea.

Back at Vimy again.

Strutting Sergeant, "Now, procedure in a very important subject.

Each group consists of a net and vice versa. A net consists of four or more stations with a central control and an efficient staff. Control is lord of all and it's absolutely imperative that his orders are followed explicitly. Do you understand?"

Voice from rear: "No, sir. Would you mind repeating that?"

Sarge: "Wake up you stupid lout! Furthermore, don't address me as, sir. I'm only an N.C.O."

Sleepy voice: "Yes, sir!"

Loud clamor from the bell. "Class dismissed."

"And this is a Lucas lamp, signaling for the purpose of, used by all formations above Brigade."

Lazy drawl: "Sorry Corporal, would you mind repeating that once more. I'm very confused."

Corporal: "Warren, describe the Lucas lamp and its function to the class."

Warren: "Sorry Corporal, I'm afraid I can't understand it either."

He would pick on me even with forty other soldiers in the class. Bothersome beggar!

"And this is a No. 9 set, M.K.4 – very simple and compact (it must have weighed about 50 lbs.) – Easy to operate when you know how."

Voice on edge of room: "Please tell it again, Staff. I'm a bit hazy on some points."

"And this is a U.C. 10 Exchange. It is in general use throughout signals. It has ten holes called jacks.

"Why don't they call them holes, staff?"

"Because, my lad, you're in the army and in here they have a different name for everything."

Parade: "Ten bodies fall out for fatigues – you and you and you."

Huge piles of coal – dirty messy job.

Thought I was to be a signal man, not a coal man. Maybe it's a course in postwar training being opened up.

Oh, well, it's only a week's work and the fresh air does taste sweet. It really makes no difference anymore. I guess I'm a soldier at last.

Guess I feel like a colt when its first broken – all messy inside.

Despite the bending and stretching, I felt fine when the week was over, proving that hard physical work never killed anyone. You learn something new every day in the army.

"How fast are you reading now, Joe?"

"Eighteen, eh? So am I. We should soon get a furlough. We've been a long time in the service now and boy, do I know it."

Captain: "Well, men, you are now qualified operators. We're proud of you. Soon you'll join your buddies overseas and we're sure you'll uphold the traditions of the signal corps and be a credit to our motto – "Velox, Versitules, Vigilantes!"

Furlough, snow everywhere – fourteen days of domestic bliss with the family. Don't want them to find out we're going overseas soon – things will be too messy when they do.

Good food, sleep, skiing and skating – freedom from want, fear and discipline is a wonderful thing.

A friend calls long distance.

"Hate to tell you this, Don, but we're all going on embarkation leave."

Ye gods, I knew it was coming – but so soon!

"Thanks, Cory,"

Very heavy feeling in stomach; damn, but it's hard to leave home. Wonder if all the fellows feel this way?

After a week, we were all back in harness ready to get the dope.

"Trained soldiers, attenshun, left wheel, quick march."

"Hey Sarge, where we goin?"

Soldier: "Haven't you heard? We're having our last medical."

Sarge: "Dummy up back there"

More lines of smelly bodies –

Medical Officer: "How do you feel" Are you ready to go overseas?"

Me: "Well, sir, I have bad eyes."

Medical Officer: "Hmmmm, is that so? They're fattening us up for the killing – guess we pull out about 2200 hours.?

Ten o'clock and we're on our way. Gosh, I feel homesick already.

Excitement mounting, big parade in full marching order, fine steak supper.

Wonder what England's like – must be pretty grim with all those bombs and things.

Wouldn't it be hell to be torpedoed on the way over?

Midnight, cold, over burdened, lonesome. Long noisy train puffing out great columns of steam into the frigid air – loud drawn out howl of the whistle.

Commanding Voice: "Everybody aboard!"

Clash of steel helmets, tired eyed men, hasty good byes, "I'll be seeing you – " peep, peep, from the brakeman and the train slowly pulled out from the siding by Fort Frontenac.

We were on our way at last – going to fight a war.

We had no sooner been seated than a Sergeant nailed me, "Warren, you're doin' guard between coaches when we go through, Montreal. We're afraid some soldiers may try to get off. Stop them by any means if they do. Get your great coat on about Cornwall. It will be cold out there."

The last was an understatement. It was frigid. Hooked again! Sometimes Fate rubs it in a bit too much.

For a long time, nothing could be heard but the click clack of the wheels on frosty rails and the occasional burst of sound from the engine as the engineer warned some late driver to get out of his way.

In the morning we were in Quebec province. All we could see were long monotonous rows of rail fences peeping their ugly heads above the snow. Miles of them, side by side, reaching like long awkward skinny arms down to the shores of the St. Lawrence.

The day wore on, and as time passed, many the face took on an unnatural flush and there were bursts of ribald song from all along the cars.

"Hey, Bob, got a bottle opener" Good show! Want a little snort? Makes you feel lots better."

"Oh, home on the range, where the deer and the antelope play."

"Hey, Harry, any Scotch left? I'm thirsty."

"Get down off that baggage rack, Mike; What in hell do you think you are? – a chickadee?"

"Oh, Canada, we stand on guard for thee."

Roar from Sarge: "Hey, youse guys, get in dem bunks – Yer disturbin de oificers in de nex car."

Darkness – silence!

At last the long train ride came to an end, and before us lay the huge harbour of Halifax.

Boats plied their careless paths hither and thither on its placid surface, and idling freighters waiting the forming of convoys sent clouds of black smoke from their warming funnels into the salty air.

It was lovely, and for a few minutes we almost forgot where we were.

Then we were at the quay, and at a long pier lay the 'Lizzy', Queen of them all.

"Cripes gang, look at that would you? Regular floating palace. Nothing small about us, I'll tell ya. Sure some change from the ships back home, eh?"

Up the long covered gang plank, full marching order, two kit bags, electric iron, soap, and what have you?

"Hey, Bill, give me a push, don't think I'll make it. Whoops, steady there. For two pins I'd heave the whole damn lot overboard."

Up long winding stairs to main deck and then down, down, down to D Deck banging on one side and then the other of the long narrow corridors. Cabin number 46 – eleven men – crowded bunks – more briefing.

It was a lovely winter's day, and having settled in as best we could, we soon had the upper decks pulsating with life.

"Wonder where our escort ships are?" I innocently asked one of the lounging sailors.

"Haven't you heard, Mac?" he came back," She don't have any – goes all the way by her lonesome."

Fine thing – the day immediately lost some of its brightness as far as I was concerned.

"Did you see that big gun up forward? Barrel on it as long as a house."

"Oh hell, what are you worried about, Warren? They say no submarine can catch her."

Fine consolation – sorry to say though it did little good. My knees were as weak as ever.

At last we were on our way. "good bye Canada, were away to fight the foe; we're sailing tomorrow, over the deep blue sea; and we can't know where we're going, but we're on our way. And I belong to Johnny Canuck, and I'm proud…

The gang planks went up and for a few minutes we crowded the rails tossing pennies to an old man below on the pier. Then we drifted slowly away as our last solid link with Canada was wiped out as surely as if we were on the far side of the world already.

There were many longing eyes watching the last bit of Canada fade away into the mist, but mine weren't among them.

"Better hide, Warren, they're looking for us to do fatigues!

Too late – "You and you and you report to the kitchen at once. It's on Deck A at the foot of "A" stairway – on the double!"

Huge platters of greasy food, semi-raw liver, cockroaches.

"Will you have some of this nice greasy bacon, Mate?"

"Why, what's the matter? You don't look well."

"Now, where's he goin' ? Sick, eh! Probably threw up all over himself. Are you goin' too?"

I tried my damnedest to get sick, even to the extent of eating everything I could get my hands on. No use! I was one of those poor victims completely immune to sea sickness. And it was the only way to get relieved of duty. Why did I have to be a small time fishing guide on civvy street? Fate again!

"Should see my boat, chum – twenty one feet of trim lines – call her Alciabiades."

"Oh, so you don't like boats, Mac – Sorry."

The third day out found us rolling in an Atlantic storm – waves racing parallel with the boat deck and I and my greasy dishes still seemingly inseparable companions.

Not even the least flicker of seasickness! Some guys seem to have all the luck.

"Whoops, whoops, whoops" – boat drill. Voice over loud speaker system: "Now everyone will fasten his life belt securely and report to his boat station at once."

There we were, packed like sardines on the boat deck, and almost as oily. Sick men all over the place and the stench of vomit holding sway over everything else.

I thought to myself there'd be few eating at supper that night, and sure enough, only about half the men showed up.

The next morning, I was taken off kitchen duty, and needless to say was very happy at no longer serving ten meals, twice a day.

Shortly after dinner the next day, we heard a welcome, "Land Ahoy" and raced upon deck to get a fleeting glimpse of Ireland through a heavy mist. It was a welcome sight and when fighter planes from Scotland came in as escorts, our cares seemed to drop from us. There were songs in the cabins that night for the first time since we had left home. Odd, the way a bit of land can bolster the spirit.

Then came a story of how we'd been sunk on the way over, but as most rumours aboard ship, it was a fable invented by some rumour monger to keep the pot stirred. It was a good joke for a while, but became staler with each telling.

Then we were going up the Clyde. Before long, green hills with toupees of purple heather on their crests began hemming us in and for some time we sailed through these pleasant surroundings gazing with eager eyes at the small red roofed cottages and stately mansions clustered here and there under their protective wings.

Greenock, small boats, little toy trains – Scotland! People waving – old woman in a garret window waiving her bloomers – Gee, do they ever look glad to see us! Mom told us there'd be days like this.

Some slick chicks over here too – may be livable after all – just give us a leave here and boy oh boy!

England next, the Midlands, long rolling plains, huge pyramids of cinders, immense chimneys. Now I know why the Scots stole the English sheep.

London at last – searchlights, roar of ack, ack, – tinkle of shrapnel on the carriage roof –

"Hey Mac, shut that blind. What the hell you think this is? A tea party?"

War, blind unreasoning hate, women and kids dying out there beneath tons of masonry – crump, crump, crump of bombs in the distance. Life sure is cheap in times like these.

Trucks, milling men, confusion – ack, ack protection, rumble of bombs – our initiation to Cove. Good meal, long dark sprawling huts ' "Spiders" – little cramped up A.T.S. bunks.

"O.K. boys, up at 9 o'clock you know. There's plenty to be done. This war can't wait forever."

"But Sarge, we just got in at 3."

"What time is it Yip?"

"4 o'clock in the morning."

"Generous as hell ain't they? – Goodnight."

More medicals, more bare asses, tattooed arms and stinky underarms.

M.O. to me: "You need glasses, do you? Can you see the big E at the top of the chart?

"Give him an A2 rating corporal – Next!"

Peace for a few days; long strolls over a quiet and interesting country side. Long fields of yellow gorse and bright shiny hedges of thorny green holly.

England does have its good points.

Basic Training again – only worse. Wonder when they'll ship us to the "field"? Demonstration squad – Princess Alice to attend – did not see orders for an early start – on Parade again – talked my way out. This life of inaction is getting damned monotonous. Do wish something would happen.

"Did you hear about that Jerry over Fleet yesterday? Machine gunned the town – two kids killed."

Damn the Germans – we'll get them yet.

"Anyone wanting a 48 hr. pass to London report to the orderly room immediately."

"Out of my way, bub, I've waited a long time for this."

At least I'll see it – London, city of valour, city of the blitz, city of hope in a world of darkness. Will the folks at home every want to hear about this! Many the soldier boy killed there in 1918, I'll betcha.

Another little train jackrabbiting along – Waterloo Station.

Smitty, Yip, Little Pud and I – what a weird combination!

"Wonder how warm beer tastes. Did you see "doc" last night stewed to the gills?"

"Lets get stinkin!"

Escalators – huge ungainly caterpillars with their human cargo coming and going from the bowels of the earth.

Rumble of deep underground coaches – tumbling, stumbling, reeking humanity all following their own little ways, doing their own little jobs, but with one idea beating increasingly between their ears – to send Adolph to his rightful place in Hell.

Brave little people! God help them!

The "Swan" – mild and bitter – bitter – mild – Tennants – Yip roaring drunk.

To sailor: "The navy stinks."

Sailor: "Yeah, so wot myte?"

Yip: "I'm gonna smack you."

Limey: "Oh, yeah!"

Smack, smack, smack – one for Yip, two for the sailor –

Sailor: "Get yer drunken chum away from ere er I'll knock his block off.."

Us: "O.K. Mac; Lets go Yip."

"Wonder where we can stay tonight? Hey mister, where is Chancery Lane? They say there's a deep air-raid shelter there."

"Can't miss it, eh? Thanks!"

Long circular metal stairs going deep into the earth – large well-lighted rooms about two hundred feet long – bunks, sheets, blankets, black tea and coffee.. Air so thick you could cut it with a knife. Hell, bed feels good – must look over the town tomorrow –

"Good night boys" – silence!

"So that's Big Ben, huh? – Clock in our town hall's as big as that."

"Ten Downing street, a dirty little hole!"

Why do we hear so much about that anyhow?

"St. Pauls – that's more like it. Just look where those bombs dropped. It's a miracle they didn't hit it."

"Seen enough? O.K. lets go back to the Swan."

Well, that's something to write home about for a while. Back to camp and those same old dirty 'spiders'.

"Did you see the look that broad gave me last night at the NAAFI dance? Almost burned by pants off – probably should develop her in my spare time – ha!"

Aldershot – town of kahki – street fights – provost, queues – "Just wait till you get to the field. It will be different there." Trip somewhat spoiled when son asked his mother, "How much is a box of matches to a Canadian?"

Twenty-six platoon, fall out and report to the orderly room for an interview. Field officer wants to see you!"

Oh happy day!

Lieutenant: "Can you operate efficiently?"

Me: "Yes sir."

Lieutenant: "How fast?"

Me: "18 word per minute accurately."

Lieutenant: "That's fine. I think you'll do. Next!"

June – "Oh what is so rare as a day in June?" –

Warm, balmy nights with a romantical looking moon.

"Hey, Warren, we're on the draft for the field. It's on the bulletin board. Yip, Stew, Milton, you and me – Mike and Joe and some of the other guys too – old home week! Hurrah! Special work too – Don't know what it is but it's very hush, hush! Kid, we've hit the jackpot!"

Another week in ye old 'spider'

Trucks, large bare sixteen-hundred weights – convoy –

Soldier: "Where are we going, Sarge?"

Sarge: "Where've you been soldier? We're headin for Leatherhead."

Soldier: "Where the hell is Leatherhead?"

Sarge: "Don't worry soldier. You'll find out soon enough!"

Leatherhead – clean, bright, old little town, cobbled streets – hill – golf course – thirty minutes to London.

Cripes, it's a lovely war!

More Morse, new Morse, strange angles – German procedures – doh-dit-doh-dit-doh! † – Long hours on search – copy, copy, copy! Crowded vans humming with alien sounds – busy intercom, V.H.F. detachments and Direction Finding with B&C Loops across the greening English Countryside – 3 Can. S.W. Section Type A.

Newly formed 3 Canadian S.W. Type A going into the field 1943

Fireworks at night as bombers dropped their loads on already burdened London and she fought back. Great grey balloons against the sky to keep the bombers high.

Now things are getting interesting! Long, enjoyable summer doing work worthwhile.

"O.K. boys, you're doin' fine. Next week you go on course to Isle of Man with British Signals."

Lovely, I hope I can't get seasick – The Irish Sea is as stormy as it's people –

Fleetwood – little Irish Sea tug, Douglas, The I.O.M. Why didn't I find this sooner?

Big Limey camp, gals and sailors everywhere, all studying Morse. "Wakey, wakey, rise and shine you Canadians" – little A.T.S. in wooden clogs preparing for breakfast (below our barracks window)

Yip dumps a water bucket on their heads and pre-dawn air turns blue. Had to pour out water, polish pails and refill every day or two.

Morse all day long up Douglas Castle way – Morse at 32 wpm at 98% correct.

The ins and outs of Kana – 50 symbols a minute – enough to drive a sane man mad. Doh, doh, dit, dit, do, dit, dit, doh, doh, dit (Zo) Barred Zebra Handigory – don't ask us what it means – "Yours is but to do and die."

British army stiff on discipline – water inside of fire buckets in the halls – drill one hour a day with ugly Sergeant Major screaming gainst the gales from the wild sea – Dances each Friday night as drafts of A.T.S. moved home to England, and their jobs at wireless stations.

October – rain, drizzly, miserable and cold – clothes wet for days on end and a disturbing cough. Can't see why people live in climates such as this. Must have aluminum lungs! Rustproof.

Nice parties with nice girls, cream of the British crop, good dances, eggs and chips and bottled beer. The more I think of England, the better I like the Isle of Man.

Seven glorious weeks! It's over now. The boat again, dead rabbits in big piles on the front deck – huge swells, sky one minute and the sea the next. Lots of warm beer and sick guys – mostly those not drinking.

Fleetwood – train station again to Rottingdean this time near Brighton.

Operations, large ungainly masts like pimples on the nose of a glorious green eyed blonde.

Eight hour shifts at singing receivers with the enemy across the wind swept channel.

Air-sea rescue – D.F. on German guns – For us the war is on.

Work was hard in the beginning, but this is worse – no margin for error – everything correct – stress, monotony at last, and drunks.

What's the world coming to?

Winter at Rottingdean – one day a storm brought a sea mine near the town, and a ship finally towed it out to sea and detonated it.

Smitty, my friend, killed as he crossed a street between a convoy of artillery guns back from a "shoot" in Wales – a barrel struck his head – and the first feeling how frail we humans are. Letters home to his family; hardest thing I'd done so far. His erstwhile happy laugh haunted for weeks to come.

On march the "schemes" to test how we would live when on the foreign shores of France – Poor meals with mutton stew, day after day.

Without a change of diet I fear that I'll sprout horns and wool.

Cook: "Lets see now. You don't appear to have lent me any money to go on leave. How about two and six?

Me: "No dice, pal! I've heard about you already."

Cook: "Well, O.K. if that's how you feel."

Little bit of stew in mess tins – thinks he can starve me into it – like Hell he will!

April and off to Folkestone, England's Hell's Corner."

Things pretty hot there – Germans over every night. Shells dropping from Calais area – ruined houses, deserted streets. Don't know whether this is good or not. High masts on cliffs beside a radar station – Channel View our house's name. "There'll be Bluebirds over, the white cliffs of Dover" – Bullshit!

See France on a clear day from our front door. Little excitement now from time to time – or is there?

Wham, bang, crack, whee – Planes over – US pilots screaming profanity – shrapnel on tile roofs –

Boys in doorways: "Did you ever see so much flack? Thought we saw ack ack at Brighton but it was nothing!"

Millions of tracers in the air – defense certainly organized! – Shell warnings little speck of silver in the searchlight's beam. – More searchlights seek it out – "Sure enough, there the bastard is!" Heavy ack ack – wham, wham, wham – the Bophors guns –

"Look, he's on fire! Here he comes down! Now, he's miles away from us."

"Crump, crump! Lucky for us he's let his bomb go in the channel. "Hurrah for good old Ack Ack batteries!"

Whump, whump, they're shelling again to night, – See the flash over there. They're Jerries biggest guns – few seconds pass – "Whump, there's another in the town. I'm glad they moved us up here on the hill."

A guy comes from the town, "Did you hear what happened? They got the "Bull." Hit the best damn pub in town!

Soldier: "Anyone hurt?"

Answer: "Yep, three killed! Just wait till we get those guys over there!"

And then there was May.

Our sets were closed down, our trucks waterproofed – looks like we're ready to invade!

Wonder will it be across here to Calais? Awful lot of truck convoys on the hill.

"Lord Haw Haw on the radio –

"So you're coming across. Why are you Canadians so silly? This isn't your war. We like you, Canadians. Think of the good Canadian blood that will be shed on our beaches. Is it worth it to die for the English?"

Dirty Brit traitor should be shot.

We do get a kick from his broadcasts, however, and the Andrews Sister's records the Germans play. However, we'll get even.

June 6 arrives – rumour has it we will be going to Normandy on June 17. Our advance party on way tomorrow.

Jerries shelled Folkestone most of the night – big convoy in Straits, large water spouts from German guns like mammoth mushrooms –

"Look, they've hit one off the point. It's on fire!"

Little toy destroyer tearing along laying great clouds of smoke – in minutes to be joined by planes building a wall of smoke between the convoy and the enemy – sleepless nights – reports on Normandy are rough!

On June 14 at 11 PM whee, whee, whee, sirens again – men crawl sheepishly from under beds – "Cripes, that guy was low – what kind of motor has that plane got? It's not a Messerschmitt I'll wager."

"Everyone outside! Sky full of ack ack – Yankee heroes raising hell behind us – little light over the Strait, ungodly roar – a hundred outboard motors joined together "What in heaven's name is that?"

Rocket guns go off down Dover way – heavies explode – light ack ack like a million fireflies, but on comes the light and the roar.

Enemy V.I. A first secret weapon!

Searchlight on it – cripes, its a small plane! Doesn't even swerve or duck – whammo – terrific blast of light – we got him – I wonder what that is.

Navy radar Sailor: "That's a new enemy secret weapon."

You're telling us!

Buzz bombs day and night – planes high above the straits on guard – "Hurricanes" best they say.

Burr roars the buzz bomb. A plane dives on it – ack ack opens up!

Blinding flash of light – "Look! The plane got him, but he's hit – dove strait through the debris." Hurricane floats down – Poor devil of a pilot. Damn the Germans!

And then to Southampton, marshalling area for Normandy – 24 hrs. in a British camp, George Formby's sister on a minute stage – and then great disappointment when we learned we must go back near

Woking for a while until the stormy Channel ran its course.

At last, early in July, about the 4th – return to Yankee marshalling area – really good food the first time in abut two years – ice cream in fact! – a convoy shrouded by night and then an L.S.T. to Normandy.

The waters black and grey with ships – the scream of diving planes – high cascades of water down along the left from German shells –

A landing in the dark sealed in the back of a small wireless truck with a stuck door – the uncertainty when it hit the shallow beach –

Torn beaches, shattered homes, first smell of death – sleep in a minefield underneath a truck and panic when we had to move next morning – the dusty road to Amblai.

Set up upon a hill beside a stream – out aerials reaching toward the threatening skies.

Our dug in quarters, well below the level of the ground – camouflage nets blending us to a hedge that hid an ancient fence – long deep slit trenches in the Norman sand – M and V rations day after day and work and plenty of it all the time – A blessing when in weeks fresh bread appeared!

Living with earphones glued upon our heads eight hours twice a day – and every night a German dropping bombs upon the beach down our small valley – the bophers gun out just behind our tent with Sinclair, Yip and I and one small mole behind those ground sheets hiding our earth walls. I almost caught him, but he was too fast – nice company! Me, two others and a mole!

Can't be choosy though. "C'est la guerre!" Guys, a couple of Kilometers up, are getting hell while we are here in relative peace and safety – but always the roaring of ten thousand guns, and summer skies aflame with tracer bullets over Caen and Maquis hunting Germans in a swamp just to our right!

One day, the famous Desert Rats rolled right through our camp, down the steep hill below and churned the stream into a muddy mess.

*Springleton and Wojanowitz in Normandy early July 1944
relaxing in front of our home near Caen*

The "flail" tanks that they had, and when they stopped to eat their rations, a cacophony of English dialects never heard before by us who marveled at their expertise with tanks and scout cars – two days later heard of heroic exploits near to Caen against the German top-notch Panzer groups.

One day three of us walked to Amblai through the dust – a miserable little town – and watched with greatest interest a group of British Soldiers in long queues waiting in wild anticipation for their turn with some abandoned women the Jerries left behind. Proud of the fact no Canadian flashes were to be seen – all little Brits. Washing our pants in a small stream itself a terrible brown.

The bouts of dysentery we had – the wasps that clustered on the breakfast food – the taste of Calvados and cider – men deathly ill – the boy from Nova Scotia, dysentery they thought, but in effect it was ruptured appendix that killed him – Maquis hunting abandoned Germans in a swamp and wanting us to help.

Five hundred planes of ours one day dropping their deadly loads near Caen, and later as our unit made its way through holes punched in the rubble of the city, the sickening sweetish smell of death in the hot air.

Caen, Falaise, Lisieux – the burned out tanks, abandoned army gear and the smell of death, always in close accompaniment – a herd of milking cattle in an orchard blown up by summer sun as big as trucks, victims of artillery duels.

And endless convoys through the devastation – standing on guard between the cab and the chassis of the truck with a Bren gun – and one eye on the wires above the road that could behead a careless person who failed to take care of oneself.

The road down to the Seine, graced by fifty burned out tanks – the targets of our rocket firing "Tiffies." Over the Seine at Pont-de-l'Arche above Rouen where fighting still went on and our enemy's major force few hours ahead – and moving fast – Maybe the war will find an ending soon – Fat chance!

One day at St. Omar, a big big scare – Digging a slit trench close beside our van – I heard the noisy clang of metal against my shovel. On hands and knees, I sifted off the sand – and there what looked like the top portion of a mine. An officer and sergeant were called – in great consternation as a private carefully dug around it and then the sheepishness when it turned out to be a disk from a disk harrow used by a farmer many years before. One takes no chances if he wants to live, as we all did.

The people in the little villages through which we passed brought out their hoarded wine to share and cheered us as we moved along our way on Canada Up. I wonder that they cheered – the devastation that we left behind.

At last we entered Belgium – land still of milk and honey – a few short miles from Ghent – historical little city of, "How they brought the good news from Aix to Ghent."

Our job to monitor the enemy still safe in Channel ports, but tightly pressed by our own troops. Our place, an orchard; was there ever any other?

First real break after those hellish weeks in Normandy – chocolate, liquor, cognac, whiskey blanc, pipes, tobacco – men on street corner shaving heads of girls who had sided with the Germans.

Joe: "Let's go to Ghent tonight! Hear there's stuff, and friendly" – Little one horse station – town.

Women everywhere, cafés well lit, soldiers everywhere – Gee, Canada has a big army! Funny you never see it when they're calling for fatigues.

Everyone smiling and happy – French floating freely through the air – holiday spirit, that's what it is! Wine flowing, leg shows – Oh my, what a lovely war it is!

ENCORE UN BEAU GARÇON QUE JE VAIS POUVOIR EMBRASSER
NOG NE SCHOONE JONGEN OM TE KUSSEN
ANOTHER NICE BOY TO KISS

A warm welcome in Brussels for Canadians

No amusement for ages and then this – from Hell to Paradise in them smooth drinks.

Sit down outside café at closing – no memory till we reach

camp – must have been some party – tam gone, R.C.C.S. flashes and badges gone, mammoth headache.

Joe: "Hey Warren, how ya feelin? You sure laid one on last night – beer, cognac and liquor don't mix, you know!"

Me: "How'd I get back here?"

Joe: "We walked, I think – all the way to Neville."

So that was why my feet were so sore!

Me: "Where did my insignia go?"

Joe: "You were in a "give away" mood – 'Souvenirs pour la petite femmes, je pense!

Be happy; we made it – Sinclair was on guard and let us sneak in – "

Home sweet home, be it ever so humble – even a lousy tent!

One day about noon we heard a steady roar coming from the west – Suddenly, the forerunners of hundreds of Dakotas towing gliders hove into view – the biggest air display we'd ever seen –

A parachute plummeted from one and dropped a motor bike right beside our camp – which a sharp officer promptly claimed for his. Must be a big attack ahead – there was. At Arnhem! That night our sets sprang to new life, and for the next week all hell broke loose in the air while we sat in comfort to register the disaster. All things passeth as did this. The channel ports were freed and we were off again.

Belgium was always a fun land for us!

"Say, Joe, do you know how to tell a city girl from a country girl?

Joe: "Nope."

Me: "O.K., here's how – see those girls on the bikes – well, if it's a city girl and the wind is blowing, she grabs her hat – not too difficult, eh?"

What corny stuff – must be good climate here for silliness and more silliness – such as the guy from Freedom Fighters with rifles and six grenades round his waist – searching for Germans who had fled long ago.

Anthwerpen – Stutter of machine gun and whine of rocket firing Tiffys (Typhoons) – like they're still clearing the air field there.

Hurrah for the air force – It must be fun shooting them down like that – Just 'burp' and they've had it. Can't help feeling sorry for them though. Nobody likes dying – know I don't like the idea any more than I ever had.

The days slip by quickly at Fort Four Antwerp.

Me: "Say Pete, what are those explosions near the harbour?"

Pete: "Just demolition squads cleaning up the area."

Explosions come closer – tinkle of shattering glass – Cripes, they must be carrying them out close to here – too close to be comfortable.

Hitler's second secret weapon –
the V designed to bring destruction to London and Antwerp in 1944–1945

Captain: "Now men, the Germans are using their new weapon, the V2 on Antwerp. You can't hear it come and you can't see it. We don't know much about it yet except that it travels 75 miles high and goes 3000 mph.

Oh, oh, sounds like Buck Rogers stuff eh?

No use worrying – if it hits – it hits – you won't even know what it was anyway!

Long nights at Fort Four broken only by explosions of V1 and V2s. Cognac galore!

"You know, Joe, the only way to stay sane in this town is to be "tight". Its not good, but after the first bottle, who cares? You can even laugh at it a little.

Joe: "Can you?"

Me: "Not really, I'm scared to death most of the time."

Macdonald spoiled it all – illicit booze bought in a downtown street and blindness.

Familiar sounds of buzz bombs and then this – it was bad enough before. Two 'doodle bugs' an hour!

"Hey, Joe, did you hear the 'boy scout' has pneumonia?"

Joe: "No, you don's say! Is it contagious?"

Me: "Not unless you like to sleep in that abandoned underpass where the Jerries use to hide a tank. They say the 'scout' moved his bed down there and it was too damp. Better the bombing than that, I'd say."

More sleepless nights. Notice that replacements were needed – volunteers dried up at home – office workers, drivers, etc. to the front. Hard days in vans with heavy traffic generated by the Schelt. The search for the illicit broadcaster sending the Jerries word of planes heading for Germany – "We seek him here, we seek him there, we seek him, seek him everywhere. Be he in Heaven or be he in Hell. That damned elusive see and tell".

We never did catch him!

Yells: "Here comes one! It's cut out! Duck!"

Heads popping from vans – officers butts sticking out from underneath tables in the Intelligence Section – Jeeze, do they look scared! Leaders of men? Hell! Give me a good domineering female any day!

Joe: "Did you hear what happened last night, Yip?

They hit a theatre in town – draggin the bodies out today. We'll see it when we're

leaving – "

Ruined theatre – sweaty dirty men – blanket covered corpses – they say 900 got it here! Quite a strain on St. Peter, I'd say – quick but effective!

They know what war is like now – hope it teaches the whole world a lesson – we don't want it any more!

One day a V2 exploded overhead and sent it's warhead into a film factory. Parts were scattered all around the unit. A hot piece of steel came through the roof of our hovel, down through two stories, and landed on my buddy's bed. I cannot remember how I reached the main floor, but assumed I jumped down an entire length of stairs. So much for adrenaline and fear!

Then out of Antwerp with its glass piled high in gutters, over the cobblestone roads – crack, squeak, bounce, creak, crack, bounce – I don't think this signal truck has any shock absorbers – either that, or the guys who made these roads had a grudge against us!

And so to Holland – only hours away – not much of a boundary here!

Breda – large forbidding woods with dilapidated hotel in middle, "O.K. boys, you're home for a while again. Set up the aerials and get to work.

More briefing – So this is the place – just like the home the major was looking for – wonder if the red-headed bugger thinks we are all as mad as he?

"Do you know where the V1 site is?" Route march for dinner – "Line up in threes about me – " Cripes, this is worse than we've had it since basic! Old Joe rejuvenated!

Rain, mud, hard work!

Mysterious white trail climbs into sky in east, "What's that, Serge?"

"Jeeze, don't know: – "Say Captain – have you any idea of what this is?

"Looks like a V2 leaving its site, doesn't it?"

Operator: "Hey, here's something funny – I picked up a signal just as Bill called out – a dit, dit, dit, dit, doh!"

Coincidence? Next day area swarming with British intelligence – questions and answers – decision that the Germans used signal to fire their missiles and that with time we could predict for London when the next V2 would come so the raid sirens could give a few seconds warning to the people.

"Let's go to town tonight, Dave? (Steele) "Long slippery march through dusk and rain – a café filled to overflowing with Polish Corp – no use us staying here – the Poles are sure in solid – well, they can have it – few glasses of coloured water, then out on cobbled street and sudden flashes in the dark across the way – a Luger, we believed –

The two of us, over a stone built fence, with me on top – poor skinny Dave beneath – Unslinging rifles, ready for to fire when down the street there roared a tiny jeep with Provost guys with guns. Two shaking operators, shivering half hidden in behind the fence –

Provost: "Where did those shots come from soldier?"

Me: "Behind the fence there just across the street."

Provost: "How many shots?"

Me: "Seven"

Provost: "He must have fired at the noise of your boots on the cobblestone – Lucky guys!"

Us: "You bet we are."

The jeep then turned around, threw a small searchlight up and down the street, but nothing there!

Me: "Can we expect this here in Breda all the time?"

Provost: "You bet, there's still collaborators here so watch yourselves."

Next day, "We're moving out to Tilburg – better place – lots of Wimmin and no Poles!"

That morning, as we left, our dispatch rider hit his loaded Sten on the short side of his own motorbike – the gun went off and put five bullets through his legs. Charged with the careless handling of a weapon, we never saw his smiling face again.

Old school in Tilburg – St. Joseph's Infirmary School of Nursing – big building – and orchard surrounded by a wall of brick – substantial place – dug slit trenches close to the building – buzz bomb alley – one in the sky every twelve minutes – and sometimes five at dusk.

Our VHF detachments on the move – "Pud", Mike and Ralph away, close to the enemy – 1000 yards for signals such as these!

One day the summons came for me to help relieve a D/F detachment between artilleries.

Pack up to leave in half an hour – good show – good to get out of here – can't stand the pace much longer – need a break.

Long ride in thirteen hundred weight – Nimegan – "That bridge over there – that's one we got from Jerry still intact without its being blown! It was a lucky break."

Reichwald forest – long somber lines of trees – fresh marks of battle –

Serge: "Now where the hell has that detachment gone? Should be about here on these coordinates – must be along this road."

Long lines of shattered trees – well churned up country road – slit trenches – scattered equipment – road broadens – concrete ahead – good show!

Big red sign 'Danger – Detour'. Now what is that for? Guess the margins must be mined, but no verge signs –

Little side road leading to the left – big field on right – wrecked village on the left.

"All out for a leak!"

Burly infantryman without insignia comes plunging up visibly agitated

"What in Hell are you guys doing here? Don't you know that trucks can't travel this road in daylight? It's under direct observation from across that field. Now, get the Hell out of here PDQ. We were just mortared 15 minutes past, and we don't need no more again. Now Scat!!!"

We scatted PDQ. Sarge was as white as a new cotton sheet, and I'm sure we were too. But one way out – the way that we'd come, and the enemy in the trees across the field!

An army truck ne'er went so fast before. Back to Tilburg, no contact with detachment – place looks like heaven now.

Impressions of the city – with its overpasses where German prisoners on flat open cars made their slow way by train towards the allies prison camps – small Holland boys with parents standing near, peeing with joy from overpass above on prisoners down below while elders laughed in glee.

Voice: "Hello, is that 3 Can S.W. signal office?

Operator: "Who's speaking?"

Voice: "Signal man Middleton."

Operator: "Oh!"

Voice: "I'm lost down town. Tell me how I get back!"

Operator: "Where are you?"

Voice: "At Army!"

Operator: "Ask anybody there."

Voice: "O.K., thank you."

One hour later – Operator: "3Can SW here."

Voice: "Do I sound any closer?"

Operator: "Who's there?"

Voice: "Middleton."

Operator: "Oh for Christ's sake, Mid. stay where you are. We'll send a truck to pick you up."

Operators are sure a queer lot at best, and as the war progresses even worse.

About time for a little touch of home – a unit dance – big night – nice plump Dutch girl to go with – that's for me.

Pleasant evening by the "Cockle" drinking chicory coffee and out staying the gloomy boyfriend – learning Dutch!

A pass to Paris, won in lottery draw – four of us from the unit, Bill and I – Lorne and "Joe". Kitbags with soap, cigarettes, all for the black market there. Drive all night long and reach Paris at dawn – drink until two and reach the Palais d'Orsay Hotel close by the Place de Concorde –

So many francs, many from the black market stores, that there was little left for us to hide in jacket pockets.

Champagne at 550F a bottle in Place d'Eve in the Pigalle – the party went till dawn – a shooting in a place behind our room – a Frenchman hit – soldiers on leave – ? no limits to this old French town.

Folies Bergere and countless French cafes plus all the famous sights we could absorb –

A rowdy start for home – through old Cambrai where father

wounded in earlier war – a machine gunner with the Princess Pats –

And back to Tilburg – with a brand new look after five days of fun.

Breakthrough in Ardennes – the Yankees in retreat – Nimegan Salient us – if Germans should reach Antwerp?

Nerves jittery for all! Now 20 men on guard out of a hundred and sixty five – issue of hand grenades, Piats and Brens – back to the infantry it seems –

Buzz bombs still over every 12 minutes you could set your clock – cold winter nights – big moon and snow –

Slit trenches dug out at 2 AM on Christmas Eve! Rum issue Christmas Day – big dinner, cognac, gin out of our hoarded stores –

On guard on Christmas night – brrrrrrt, wham – Bren guns, Stens and rifles in the eerie night – Sounds like our front has opened up at last!

Rumored the Deutch to drop in parachutes here – tonight – and few men sober. What a place for us to be! Rae shooting with a Bren at Dutchman's bathroom window showing lights!

The wham, wham, wham of Bophers signaling a drop, men rushing here and there in the resounding dark – in fifteen minutes 10,000 men fall out – how trained we are!

But it's a false alarm, and soon we're back to camp, all glad it was but a bum steer.

Orders from Army for our unit to fall back to safety in Belgium. Gould, Warren etc. will remain behind with VHF to monitor their tanks! A rear guard action! And friendly Hollanders, now depressed and dumb no longer friends it seemed –

One night on duty marching near a wall between machine gun post strategic placed, four well known posts in open field began to move, "Halt! Who goes there?" No answer and then shots. How stupid I did feel – and all agreed.

Shut in a little room with five good men – no going out – we'd hide as best we could – and listen for the guttural sound of German voices on the moving air – tank traffic less than some 3000 yards! And fear each time a noise came from outside!

A few short days, and then the welcome sound of units coming back – The Ardennes broken, Germans on the run – thank God!

And then there seemed no warning of a strike! Were operators hedging on their jobs because of pay? A simple answer given, the enemy had gone to landline, just before the battle had begun.

Two months of easy calm ensued. And aiding Holland friends I met steal a pig, and scrape it in the night on a back porch and "Jo and "Spitfire" and the mother who brought headcheese for me once or twice a week to compounds gate to every ones surprise!

The growing hordes of soldiers in the town – our cook who shot a young girl in the leg all for a refused kiss – how thin he was when he came back to us from 100 hours drill on double with great pack filled with 60lbs of sand.

And at an army show one night, hundreds of soldiers having pay books checked for deserters by scowling military cops –

We knew the drive was coming to the Rhine. On New Year's, last kick of Luftwaffe overhead strafing long convoys on the Tilburg road 500 yards away – an unsuccessful one as it turned out and lost, the German air force that we'd see.

Scottish nights and English rights – huge queues for Cinema – men swirling like a colony of ants!

Then moving to Nimegan – dilapidated school out near the famous bridge. Artillery spotting post in upper room – batteries all around us – wham, wham, wham – poor place to catch some sleep with threat of our foe down below the hill on night patrol across the flooded Waal.

The ambulances returning from the strife near Cleve, Calcon and Wessel – more hours of the unending work – the last push comes at last! A moving up – the artificial fog – was hard to see your hand before your face – rumble of tanks – sporadic burst of guns – incessant battery of the eardrums with heavy interference in the air – communications poor! Long messages to send, God knows what where?

At eight o'clock one night all Hell busts loose – a steady pounding of artillery, whine of the Tiffys going over – cacophony of 14000 guns heard eighty miles away – in Groningen, across the bridge to Arnhem and the mass of destroyed houses from the last battle of the weeks before.

Our final battle weary move toward the Rhine – Through Arnhem with its rubble laden streets and ruined houses three sided near the roads – the furnishing like dolls made clear three stories high to us who passed below.

Long lines of 'buffaloes' moving toward the enemy – landing crafts – infantry. Sure pity the first lot!

10:00 hrs – the infantry across at Emmoch with paratroopers over and the Germans falling back –

Order by Ike , "We shall press on until the end." Long miles of convoys slowly moving up and ordered to the verge to make the way for priorities of fuel to feed the hungry tanks –

The harried officers and haggard wounded soldiers coming back – I wonder if its worth it?

And off again through ruined German towns across the Rhine at last – my God its worse than Caen with not a wall over six feet high left up – piles of gray rubble – one landmark only left – a standing chimney flaunting a shell hole high above the ground teetering precariously over the other ruins – this ought to teach aggressors something now.

In and out of Holland once again and then to Meppen – our huddle of tents in a large flat open field and Rain – waking in morning to a little stream of water through the tent and blankets wet and cold –

Another move – our trucks bogged down to axles in the mud – at last a 'gypsy' camp on a high hill along the edge of forest –

Deer hunting out the front flap of the tent – The Kaiser's deer – the size of white tail fawns on trails at home – fine camping trip with the enemy day and night on his last move – the war is quickly rolling to an end.

A burying mound close by with many Polish workers buried

there!

Me: "Lets go hunting. Dave."

Dave: "O.K. , I'll get my gun."

Long tramp through the spring woods which smell of home. "What's that?" "Looks as though the Germans had a camp!" High barbed wire fence lost in the brush – "Let's look around a bit".

"Aha, what's this?" Small car and motorcycle hidden well – good business – thorough smashing job – "Bet they won't ever use this stuff again!"

"What a funny looking spot right over there!" Get a long stick and push away the leaves – a box, and buried in the earth, just like a summer camper's ice box was at home –

"Hey Dave, come here! I think we've hit the jackpot." And we had – twelve dusty bottles beautiful to our eyes – one of Champagne – an 1800's date – red wine, cognac and liquors – God, what a cache!

We finish the champagne and then try a liquor that tastes like licorice stick. Dave has some tracers for his rifle and, placing the bottle gainst a nearby tree, smashes it all to hell. We stagger back to camp with unused bottles bulging out our jackets. We'd had all we could hold – and more! Camp, supper – blackout for me! Next morning having missed my first real scheduled shift since Normandy. Somewhat upset – Gee whiz talk about dynamite – we should have known that stuff would have a kick. Where did the rest go? So the guys relieved us of our load and saved our shift – great gang! and drank our booze!" Why did I feel so lousy?

At 1100 hrs. that day the word came through the war in Germany was at an end – men tumbling from vans – cheering and shaking hands – the trail had finally ended for us all – Old Joe and men returning from the town with loads of Schnapps – "Yip" down on the highway flogging down a convoy, giving the good news – collecting goodies from the happy crews – officers sharing at last their personal hoards – Huge fire at night with R.I. searching for his uppers on the bushy hill.

Now maybe we'll get home! O Canada!

But there were things to come – in two days time our work began again to monitor disbursing German armies in the north –

One day on a return from Meppen saw the ultimate in tragedy – three British soldiers near a proposed overpass defusing land mines meant to kill a ton – a faulty move – and "wham" – three men destroyed in seconds, little of them left – the irony, all set for home, and then a terrible end.

Good for us though! Reminded at the iffiness of life, we'd not relax our vigilance just yet!

The German youngsters coming to our camp, pleading to be our prisoners of war – and being sent away – their terror of the Russian victory in the East.

The rule forbidding us to talk to civilian folks – upon the threat of German occupation if we did.

R.I. down at the little river shooting corks from wine bottles we'd let go upstream – impressing frauleins with his steady aim and then return to Holland and two little towns Angelo and Hengelo for a final swing as forces of the enemy broke up –

To Apeldoorn – our work finished at last – disbanding after years of camaraderie and stationed to units readying for home.

A couple of us sent to Groningen – a tent camp in a park – the children begging for left-over food and us, supplying all we could.

The Holland friends we met – now peacetime friends – and how they took us freely in their homes – my friends, the Englehardts among the best – and Enno and his struggling with our language – learning fast.

That summer, time hung heavy on our hands – A trip to England taking German prisoners – a 3 day visit on the British shores.

Twenty-seven men and officers – a 60 hundred weight. – Woody and I in back with bayonets fixed – picking them up near Clive – a night at Diest near Brussels where the worst of German prisoners were kept – the crowd of Belgians gathering round a German Pee break on the road – a freedom night at Ostend while our men were guarded by a British company and then the L.S.T. to Tilbury on the mighty river Thames – The British Red Caps waiting at the dock, one for each prisoner we four had brought for three days through the war broken land –

We laughed as did the Germans at this act! – Three short days leave in London and then, the long trip back to Apeldoorn again.

Boredom set in – God knows when at last we will get home. What can be done to hasten up the time? So back to school in Ghent for three short months to study science subjects – and have fun – the professors each day surprised to find their classroom skeleton within the tall glass case smoking a cigarette in one hand casually – next day a pack of gum! And how we liked those tricks –

Don and friend near the College of Ghent on course Autumn 1945

Ghent not the lovely town we'd earlier seen, but war had passed her over and now conditions there were grim – shortage of food, and drink and goods within the stores – the people glum and quite dependent – t'was good to end the course and head back north.

More waiting for the call to go back home – short five day leaves to visit Amsterdam – was there when the Bomb was dropped on

Hiroshima and we cheered – black market at its height – and fourteen days in Paris, Lorne and I – contact with pen-pal friends before the war and seeing Paris as it should be seen – my second trip – A final effort to the British, Isle of Man, to say goodbye – and finally back to England for return to where our hearts were – with 5th Div.

A final leave in Edinburgh, Scots want to become nation. New Years with friends who desired nothing more than going it alone.

At last to Southampton and the 'Lizzy' waiting there – held up, we knew not why until the flashing bulbs gave us a clue, that far below our deck a celebrity was coming with us on the ride across the cold Atlantic – and "Who is it?" "Churchill, the Saviour of the West!"

This time, no extra work – how soon one learns the places one can hide to miss fatigues – thousands of men on board – and poker games galore as fortunes soon changed hands.

A winters storm – and Churchill's short address to all we troops huddled below his deck – his incoherent talk – brandy we whispered – until they turned off the P.A.

Finally, the outline of New York with the Statue of Liberty – and boats and bands and water hissing high into the sky – Grand Central Station late at night some hundreds of us – kit bags and great packs – rifles and souvenirs – a winter train puffing its clouds of steam across the ice bound land to Canada – and at nine o'clock next night to Kingston station and the sight of war-aged parents waiting in the cold with anxious eyes and brother and sister who I hardly knew and Chaffey's Lock the circle closed at last.

And the old House upon the Hill, serene and smiling in the January sun.

Rideau Reflections

And as a boy, I loved it.
The clear blue sky
Reflected on the shining surface
Of the lakes –
The old stone house,
Resplendent on the hill,
Our home.
The mysteries of wooded hills;
The B.B. gun,
A father's gift at eight –
The first fat partridge
Behind Wilf Regan's barn –
Upon a cedar bough it sat and gazed
Thinking itself well hid;
While I, feeling a new found power
In the gun
Took careful aim
And shot it through the head.
How proud I was!
The fishing rod;
An antique version,
With two-handed grip –
Running with eager feet
To the old dock
Which stretched
Pale grey above the upper gates
To filch a minnow from George Taylor's boat

Aged and greasy, smelling of stale bread
And piled at back
With heaps of glistening nets.
The dew hung heavy on the morning grass
As wealthy anglers
With rods of split bamboo,
A poor boy's dream,
Came leisurely
Down the short gravel path
From the Hotel
Decked out in princely clothes
For the day's sport.
The motorboats,
Painted their greens and white
Sporting long tows of skiffs
Which bobbed and wove
In the clear water –
"Letitia"
The old "Tin Tub"
Tied tight along the wharf
While guides,
Skin leathery from long hours in the sun,
Stuffed stubby pipes
Blinked at the sun, and talked.
One, Bob Lasha,
His massive head of white,
Knee britches,
Golf socks,
Sneakers on his feet,
Carried a basket bigger than himself
And chuckled in his quiet, friendly way.
And "Clinter",
Kicker tied
To bow of battered skiff,
Felt hat perched jauntily

On grizzled head,
Recounted to the listening skeptics how
With hand-made cedar rod
He each day hung
Limits of massive Big Mouths
From the tips
Of overhanging cedars
Near the shore.
While I, by the great pails of bait
That lay
Deep in the morning waters,
Hooked my black bass
Yet envied them their sport.
Well before eight
The Locks ground to new life.
The guides with boats below
Felt that the waters "Up Above" surpassed,
And met those "Up Above"
On the way down.
The lockmen,
Herm and Ned,
Envying the fishermen
I'm sure, as much as I.
Cranked at the crabs,
And sweat and swore a little,
Disgusted with the vagaries of man.
Old "Daisy",
Milked early at the barn,
Was led to pasture
Where she spent her solitary days,
Relieved but once a year
By a mysterious trek
To Simmon's farm
For purposes unknown.
At nine the lock was empty –

The old grey skiff,
A world of turtles, pollywogs and snakes
Explorer's paradise.
The weeds, heavy and thick
Smelling of fish and watery decay –
Opinicon!
Behind the "Boathouse" point
An ancient moss back,
Weighed twenty pounds at least,
Sold for a quarter
To the Hotel cook –
A fortune to be gambled with
And lost –
The slot machine
Gorging its hungry innards on my wealth.
The swim,
Tag on the lock,
Wild racing up the gates,
The thrill
Of plunging in the current
At its height.
The flume,
Dark weather-beaten planks
Worn by long years of water,
Old in my father's youth.
With silver eels
Caught in its weathered grip
To chase and corner
Down by the deep trap's end.
The mysteries
That lurked about the Mill
All dark and silent,
Haunted at high noon.
And will-o-wisps at night
Across the "drowned land"

South west from the lock
With Joe,
Two long light poles,
First bull-head fishing of an early spring
Before us in the dimness, myriad stumps
Weird outlines
In the evenings gathering gloom
Mysterious light
The night call of a loon
And two small boys
A mile away from home
Strange thoughts of sudden death to follow
Haunted my every hour
With tales of banshees
Knocking on the pipes,
Pictures awry,
And prophesizing dream
The carbide lights
That flared
And threw strange shadows
On the wavering walls.
The whisper of the mice's feet that passed
To hidden nests,
Deep in their ancient maze –
A scream,
Late in the night
Out in the hired girl's room –
A wisp of moonlight
Stealing cross the floor?
The sound of footsteps
In an upstairs hall
With no one there,
Feeding the fear
Into a senseless, overwhelming thing
That felt a Presence

In the gloomy rooms.

And school two miles away –
With tall Bill Gifford
Hurrying us along.
First day –
Miss Simmons
Then Miss Gourlay,
Happy souls!
Eight classes in one room –
Recess and "Kick the Stick",
The carving on the desks,
The musty smell of children,
The great stove,
That roared and sputtered
Belly glowing red –
Hot lunch,
Cocoa or pork and beans
Prepared by pupils hands
And none too clean –
Cowboys and Indians in the lower swamp –
An old pine tree
With limbs a boy could grasp
And swing aloft
To see the endless world
Of swaying tree tops
In the restless breeze.

An old ash rail
Provided a first smoke,
And teachers supple arm
Five times
With the old schoolhouse strap
Made us both wince
But never once draw back.

At springtime recess
The fast run
To Rowswell's Creek
Down the well beaten path
Through whispering pines –
A mother partridge
Leading us astray –
And pike that swirled
And rippled the deep pool
Below the mutter
Of the spray drenched falls –
The pond behind the school –
Clubs and a rusty can
Shinny –
Ice glare and sweet
As any boy could dream –
On Saturday's the lake,
First freeze,
The fish
Caught in the shallow bays
Swam underneath the ice,
Clear as a new-washed glass,
Darting in haste
As we sped from above.

Bright happy sounds were there
As sparking as the skies.
The ringing of the axe
Into hard wood;
The crosscut saw
With its rhythemetic rasp;
The thunder of the elm tree as it fell.
Old "Dick" and "Jack"
Their nostrils spouting jets
Of silver steam,

Tossed high their heads,
Rattled their bits,
And moved their mighty load.

Out on the lake
As winter spread his grip,
Jim Simmons
With a little band of men
Close-buttoned and high-booted
For the work,
Harvested ice,
A hundred pounds a cake,
Soft snow on top
Clear crystal blue beneath.

The euchre games,
Good neighbours dropping in,
Grouped round the kitchen table
While the wind
Whistled about
The blustering ice-bound eves.
Faces intent
And fingers stiff with toil
They shuffled out
The long, cold winter nights –
John Dorey, going it "alone"
With greatest glee –
Up from his chair
Eyes glistening,
Hair on end,
Beating the table
With his massive fist,
As cards flicked out
And all but his partners
Smiled.

Then, as the clock,
Proud on the kitchen shelf
Tolled out the midnight hour,
Boiled tea,
Beef sandwiches,
And cake,
Soon took away the taste
Of a defeat.

Some nights
The moon played coldly
On the glittering lakes
And cast long shadows
On the wintry shores.
The boom of ice
Up heaving in the still
Dwarfing the crackle
Of the maple logs
Which flamed
Deep in the stove
Beside the bedroom stairs.
And boys grow up
And search the distant recess
Of the soul
To catch a glimmer
Of that vanished joy.

And as a youth I loved it –
The noisy, busy Lock,
But missing now
The Buenovistas scream,
And many friendly faces of the past.
The old grey flume
Had vanished with the tide
Of busy man

Seeking his destiny,
But Tim,
His old felt hat
Anchored in place
Upon his greying hair,
His straight brown pipe,
Clenched in his stubborn jaw,
Had winter tales
To stir the vagrant blood.
In rocking chair
Close by the roaring fire
He wove his spell
As a magician can
With tales of hunting parties
In the north –
The trip on Whitefish Lake
When from his boat
The wounded buck
Rose to his feet
And dove
In action
Quicker than a wink
Over the starboard side –
How he in desperation
Roped the beast
Tight to the old punts stern
And used it as a motor
To the shore.

Of rafting blue bills,
Sharp at the hour of eight
Leaping as one
Into the fluttering sky
And seeking out his decoys
Near the "blind" –

The trout from Devil Lake
That won the prize
For all the Northern region –
And the room,
But for the ticking of the kitchen clock,
Hushed –
And became the dusky forest trails
Through which we travelled,
Each, his separate way.

In March –
Soft slushy days
And frigid nights –
The sleigh tracks
Through the sprawling
Maple groves –
And buckets
Brimmed to full
With sparkling sap
Brought us all eager
To the sugar shack
Which puffed
A steady cloud
Of fragrant steam
Into the frosty air.
And George was there –
His Club stained chin
Sporting a three days growth
Of hoary beard –
Red cotton shirt
Crossed braces on his back
Bent like a demon
Near the roaring fire
And deftly swept
A mass of creamy foam

From out
the Bubbling cauldron
Of the vats –
An expert in the art –

When April
Honeycombed
The southern slopes,
And left dark shadows
On deep rutted roads
With ancient Ford
And makeshift clattering saw
The "sawyers" came
The high piled rollway
Close beside the pump-
Completion of a grueling winter's work
In Hughson's swamp
At eight o'clock
The motors stuttering roar
Dispelled the magic
Of the crow loud morn,
Its glittering blade
Biting the fragrant
Birch, and elm and oak
Rasped out its heathen song
To turquoise skies.
The seven men
With leather-mittened hands,
Grasped, as a team,
The frosty dull grey logs
And stalking with slow steps
Moved to the hungry blade.
And Frank,
With little laughing crows feet
At his eyes,

Cuddled his snuff
And dodged the singing steel
Beside the busy apron
Tossed out blocks
Just sixteen inches long
On foot-stained snow.
At noon
The neighbouring women
Spread a feast
That brought delight
To every workman's eye.
Then my first job –
Opinicon, my love,
The old grey skiff
Five miles at six o'clock
Fish all day long
Back to the Locks at nine –
Three dollars for my labour,
Nothing more.
Too hard, my mother said,
But I,
With youth's enthusiasm
Loved it all.
One day on Sand
When clouds piled in the north
As black as night
Our motor boat broke loose
And we,
With lightning streaming round
Wet as swamp rats,
Yet conquering our fear,
Launched a frail craft
And saved it from the rocks.

Wall tents that sprouted

On green summer Points
"First come – First served"
After the snow had gone
Ashbaughs and Virrs,
Cordes and MacIntyre
Bringing new cultures
And the winds of change
The nests of black snakes
On the Old Mill Point
And Acton's cottage
With its curious pets –
The Lisse girls
And their sweet harmonies
At campfires on the Point
When shadows came
And bringing us
Soul satisfying peace
One quiet summer evening
A girl "streaked"
Straight across the Lock
And left its keepers
Bug eyed
For a week.
And the green bass
Suspended in the current
By the mill
Daring us all
To catch them if we could.
The small informal gatherings
On Lock hill
To while away
The balmy summer eves
With wholesome talk and argument
'Til ten
When Herm declared "Good night",

And went to bed.
The time the fishing guides
Were forced to move
To the Bull Pasture
By the new built hall
Too party-minded
For the tourist crowd.
Democracy at work????

On Saturdays the dance –
Clean shirt
Shoes on the feet,
Blue jeans –
The first few faltering steps
In the new hall
The "Clear the Floor",
And "Orders for a Square"
Girls in light summer dresses,
Sparkling eyes,
And feet that tapped the rhythm
In suspense.
Four ample matrons
Guarded well that hall.
Jenny, with fair Scot's face,
Enthroned on a chair
Sat like an ancient queen,
Feet firmly set,
Her needles flying fast;
Scarlet of hue,
Scanning the happy crowd.
And Alice, Fran and Hazel
Hawkish eyes
Each on a different sector
Of the floor
Brought quick disgrace

To any youngster who
Revealed inebriation
In their sight.
The little groups of boys
In noble isolation
By the door-
The "Choose your Partners",
"Everybody Swing" –
Brown arms,
Slim waists
And then the dripping brow.
And so the fleeting summer season passed,
And maples turned
Their autumn glory on.
The old familiar school was left behind.
Life's pulse beat slower
In a second home.
Cribbage with Cliff –
Long hours spent
To train the stubborn mind...
The overwhelming strangeness of it all!
Doughnuts for breakfast,
Oyster in the shell,
The smell of new singed hair,
The three-act play,
And Ella,
With her quiet, peaceful smile
Back from the latest funeral to face
Her husband's scorn
With dinner minutes late.

But always at the end
The waiting Lock
On weekends
In the glorious autumn sun.

The old ten-gauge
And I,
Waking at four
To creep
Out of the sleeping house
Down to the shadowy marsh.
The whisper of the mallard's wings
On high o'er head –
The muted splashing
Of a cautious oar,
And trembling agitation in the "blind"
Waiting for light –
How gradually it came!
At last, the booming
Of the anxious guns,
And sun, turning to gold
The sudden autumn shores.
Cold winter nights –
The crunch of frigid snow
Under our eager feet.
The bobsled runners
Whispering down the hills.
One night the sleet came
Much to all our joy
Turning the roads
Into a shining ribbon
Through the town.
Next morning, there was paradise on earth.
The countryside,
A diamond in the sun.

And the school bus –
An ancient run down car
The pleasure we all had
When Allie swore –

A master of the art –
The day that Lindsey Smith
Helped by a little band
Of eager "hands"
Prepared a soap-can bomb
And set it off –
Rattling the windows
Of the old brick school.
And in the background
Sounds of war –
A madman's raving voice –
What need of books
Let's live it while we can!

That summer in the heat –
The railway track –
An extra gang –
Long metal tongs.
Bunched muscles –
Bloody hands.
Sun in long cuts
So hot
It dulled the brain –
And six o'clock
A million years away –
But every night,
The Lock,
Old in its quiet wisdom
Balmed the wounds,
And sent us out
Fresh to another day

And in those years, I loved it
Though apart,
With aching bitterness

One only feels
When separation is a senseless thing.
Great Khaki mobs,
Excitement at its height,
Long lines of boys
Waiting a morning meal,
And hectic hours
With guns and maps
And all those alien things
That one must learn, to fight.
The "poker" –
Face of young Canada,
Wild, and tough, and proud,
Showing her warrior spirit
To the world.

One midnight
In the winter's bitter cold,
Shrouded in clouds
Of noisy puffing steam,
Huddled in great coats
Shapeless in the mist
The "Draft"
A thousand strong
Moved to a railway spur,
Stumbled inside a troop train,
And began
The journey
Into areas unknown.

Trip to the coast,
The "Lizzy" waiting there
Steel grey

With mighty guns
Trained on the leaden skies
The fifteen thousand men
Deep in her teeming innards
Now aware
That all those sights
Mountain, lake,
Field and stream and plain
Old Locks of ancient stone
Might be forever
Vanished from their sight.

The air raids over London –
Drawn faces in the gloom,
And shrapnel's rattle
On a cobbled street.
The dim lit "pub"
Where everybody sang
And hope soared high
To vanish with the dawn
The endless days
Of waiting for the Drive
That never seemed to come.

Cove, Leatherhead,
Rottingdean,
Folkstone,
Douglas, the Isle of Man –
A dim parade of faces
Through the mists –
Harold and "Yip"
Stewart and Lorne and "Joe"
Short leaves in Scotland,
Winter on the coast –
Pub of "The Valiant Sailor"

On the hill –
That spring
The gorse was yellow
On the cliffs –
Below, the restless waters
Of the Strait,
"Mosquitoes" playing leap-frog
On their crests.

One day
A plodding convoy
Dared the wrath
Of big German guns
And came our way –
Moving with indomitable pride
While feathery columns
Blossomed in their wake.
And we,
Detached and silent on the cliffs
Envied the taste of battle
That was theirs.
Finally it came –
Southampton, marshalling area
For the force
That rocked the world
One sunny summer morn.
Woods roared to life,
Long lines of Khaki men
Said their last prayers
Some waved a fond farewell
And vanished
In the bloody haze of strife –
All day the sky
Echoed the growling mutter of the land
As row on row

THE HOUSE ON THE HILL | *Don Warren*

Vast aerial fleets
Swept by,
Our night
A rain of death
Fell on the beach,
And sky
Became a living thing to fear.

Caen and Falaise,
The crossing of the Seine,
Long convoys on the move
Day after day
Under the burning sun.
St. Omar, Ghent,
And Antwerp –
The V.I.
That roared at night
Across the star-decked sky.
Breda, and sudden shots
The Luger's flash
A moment's panic
Crouched behind a wall.
Tilburg, Nimegan
And the long hard road
Down to the murky waters
Of the Rhine.

And through it all
Dreams of the Lock,
Leeds County in the spring,
The cool green shores,
The waters of the bay
Where fishes splashed
And lonely loons
Shattered the slumbering night,

Intensifying
As the days blurred by
The will
To see again
The tossing maple trees
Decked in their autumn splendour
On the hills.

And then the end,
Crouched on a wooded slope
Beside the Ems –
Wild celebrations,
Whisky from tin cups
The numbness of care-vacated mind –
Slow light returning
To war hardened eyes-
And thoughts of home
And friends
And places dear.

Those months of killing time –
Groningen, Brussels, Paris
Antwerp and Amsterdam –
Short five day leaves
To visit Holland friends –
Last trip across the Channel,
Dover bound –
And London with her lights –
Already strange.

Southampton
Mighty "Liz"
All battle tired and proud –
Long slow green waves
Tossing their foam swept crests –

Churchill aboard,
The saviour of the West –
Statue of Liberty
Tugboats and welcoming bands –
Comrades dispersing,
Quick, fond, sad farewells,
As troop-trains crawled
Towards a thousand towns
O'er ice gripped land.
And then —————
The welcoming arms
Of war-aged parents –
And the Lock
Solid, serene, secure,
And smiling
In the January sun.

Morning Shoot

The dawn breaks grey.
The wind is cold.
Across the steaming marshes
Little cats-paws of steam rise up.
Men huddle in the reed blinds
And murmur of past hunts.

A few yards out-dim silhouettes
The decoys bob and weave
In tireless circling agitation,
The Judas of their kind.

With growing whisper
Our of deep lowering skies
Comes faint the whisper of a thousand wings
The decoys pause in hushed expectancy.

With grating overtones
Of artificial man-made things
The deep quack, quacking
Of a duck at feed
Rides loud and clear the wind.

From high above
On swooshing crescent wings
Thin triangles dip down
At undetermined speeds

Bluebills flash overhead.

In rapid fire staccato
Hot guns boom out
Grim messages of death.
Soft bodies strew dark waters.
White streaks show swimming dogs,
Whose barks ring through the marsh.

Slowly, men stretch cramped limbs
The smell of bottled coffee fills the air.
Outboards whine into life.
The morning flight is done.

SUMMER STORM

Dark grows the sky
With little rustlings in the poplars
The south wind heralds rain.
The robins in the maples
Swell out their throats
In rhapsodies of joy
A crow scoots furtive from a farmer's field
To deepest sanctuary in the woods
And in the background
Thunder.

The tempo rises
The wind comes in short gusts
Lifting the dust in little swirling clouds.
From time to time
In lowering skies
The lightning's flash
And thunder shakes the earth.

Down by the lake
The leaping madcap waves
Reach high upon the shore;
And farther out, the rain
Obliterates the indistinct
And threshing wall of trees.

By Brady's Point, an elm,

Touching its toes
Falls flat upon its face,
Its head
In the dark waters.

Flash after flash
Lights up hand-reaching sky.
The wind whips through the trees
As one by one
We huddle in the shelter of the hut.

Then it is over.
A little patch of Dutchman's blue
Shines through
Far in the misty south.
The thunder dies
The rains recede;
The lake resumes
Its blue and placid role,
And we move out
Breathing the freshness
Of the rain washed air
And go in slow content
About our chores.

Spring

Spring is that glorious season
'Fore summer spreads over the earth
When young things make love without reason
And sing out their laughter and mirth

When blossoms pop out in the orchard
And birds make their nests in the trees
And the frogs in the meadows are croaking
Where the water has made little seas.

A time when the farmer is digging
The holes for his cabbage and beans
And the crows in the pine woods are calling
For they know what the fine weather means.

Its the season when nature is wakening
From its long sleep in under the snow
When the cold from the good earth is banished
And summer is coming we know.

HOME

From out the glass paned window of my room
Where oft with idle pen I sit alone
I hear the wind outside my haven croon
And it reminds me of my country home
Of mother, sister, father, brother, all
That helps to make my world so bright and small.

The old stone house, my home upon the hill
Which for a hundred years has fought the chill
Of bitter winters, drought wrought summers, dreary falls
And has not yet succeeded to Fates call –
It holds a place so sacred in my heart
that only death can draw we two apart.
Its ancient walls wherein I once did play
Will never from my memory break away

Chaffey's Locks

When the summer wind is blowing
Then its time I was a going
Back to lands where fishes play
Break the glassy stretch of bay
Where the waters ever blue
Reach out cooling arms to you
Busy boats throng round the docks
At Earth's paradise – Chaffey's Lock
Where the campfires beam at night
Casting out their fitful light
On the young folks gathered round
Sprawled out on the clean green ground
In the embers of the fire
Burned to darkness almost dire
Wieners done to very twist
Wait the touch of hungry lips
All this can be found right here
At Chaffey's Locks this very year
The soft low voices of the throng
Help pass the evenings right along
And if you're there a month or day
You never will regret your stay
With people who are really kind
No better on this earth you'll find
So come to Chaffey's Locks this year
You'll certainly derive much cheer.

VACATION

Oh, its great to be happy and free
Like the whales and fish in the sea,
Where you haven't a care,
And the soft summer airs
Tells of pleasures there are still to be.

When the sun bobbles up in the east,
You arise without caring the least,
And as birds chirp a song
You go gliding along
Under clouds that are whiter than fleece.

The fishes all wiggle and play
And break the smooth surface of bay
The motor boat roars
You're out from the shore
And laughing you're gaily away.

The fish hawks from forests come up
And they dive and they roll and they duck
Round the place where you anchor
Set up such a clamor
And needless to say there's poor luck.

But fishing's not all in the art,
It depends on the state of the heart
If the fishes won't bite

Don't forget that they might
And there's plenty worse places to park

So just come to old Chaffey's each year
And pull your boat up to the pier
You will get a fine tan
And you may get a man
Whether you want one or not.

LATE SPRING

The ice was late in going out this year
For days, the lakes
In solemn spectral black
Lay motionless and still.
The sun rose cold
Passed cold across the sky
And coldly set.
No robin came
To warm our winter hearts
With his bright song.
The marsh stood bleak and silent,
And little patches of coarse snow
Defaced the northern slope
Of each brown hill.
And then,
One day at dawn
We heard the "Caw"
of nature's messenger –
And knew at once
Springtime
Was on its way.

PEACEFUL NIGHT

The light is low, low flickers the dim fire
In grates of blackened stones,
Unbroken is the silence, still the noisy screeching,
Of the winters wind,
Softly, silently steals the moon's sad rays
Through heavy masses of low hanging clouds,
Wrapping in icy splendour like a ghostly cloak
Our happy country homes.

Across the ice bound lake a groaning
Like some poor mortal in supreme distress,
It fades and gleams, and fades and gleams again,
And then it dies along the misty shore,
And clothes it in a rich and golden shroud.

CONTENTMENT

Soft swaying fronds against a wintry sky,
Appealing arms stretched upwards to the stars,
From distant swamp the hoot owl's mournful cry,
Faint answering echoes floating from afar,
The sheen of golden moonlight on the bay,
The twinkle of a million stars at play
      Appease me.

The frosty stream of breath trails in the air,
The crunching of my footsteps in the snow,
Aurora Borealis' sudden flare,
The way the flickering shadows come and go,
The passing teamster's sudden burst of song,
The way the icy runners glide along.
      Pacify me.

The tinkle of a little brook nearby,
Wending its lonely way toward the sea,
The mighty north wind's gentle freezing sigh,
Meandering softly through the snow wrapt trees,
The absence of the cannon's shattering roar,
Assurance that it will be heard no more.
      Contents me.

Contentment is the greatest thing in life,
It springs from many sources great and small,
For some it comes in sound of bloody strife,

For others in Fame's lofty gilded hall,
I would not change my life for that of Kings
Enough for me the song my pencil sings.
      Believe me.

Bull-Heading

Sitting in my little boat
Hear the breezes sigh
See the tiny fairy fires
Flickering in the sky.

Smell the tang of balsam
Wafting from the shore
Lazy lapping waters
"Gainst my dangling oars.

Seeping through the evening mist
Eerie 'gainst the moon
Comes the lingering mating call
Of the lonely loon.

In the murky darkness
Crowding close around
Wells a froggy chorus
From the marshy ground.

Here I sit a fishing
Waiting for a bite
Really doesn't matter
It's a perfect night.

Sunset

Sunset – the word conveys to me
That I shall soon be free,
Free as the robin piping in the tree overhead
One more short night, then what?
I do not know.
But He who guides our course across sweet life can tell,
He knoweth that path well.
And he will guide my steps
O'er that long path of life and death
And lift me, when I stumble o'er some rock,
Which set unwittingly in my way
Tries oh so hard, to lead me far astray.

Sunset – the golden ball of fire
Hangs wavering in the west
Fringed 'round with fleecy clouds.
It sinks, its golden banners fade,
'Tis night, silent, mysterious night
That clothes our weary world in welcome slumber
A solitary robin calls to mate upon hidden branch
He's quiet now also.
With penetrating fragrance the flowers close
Their multi coloured petals.
House lights pop on like fireflies.
Night reigns supreme.

BALLAD OF PETER MILAN
(any references purely imaginary)

I
From across the groanin. ice field
Comes a long blood curdlin' cry
'Tis a sound I shall remember
Till the very day I die.

II
Let me tell you how it happened
How this story came to be,
Why his restless spirit haunts me,
Miles and miles across the sea.

III
Pete Milan was a dentist
Just a good home lovin' lad,
Had a cottage, was his castle,
Never dreamed his wife was bad

IV
Met her at a dance one evenin'
Told me she was young and free
Asked if I would take her walkin'
Said she liked no one like me.

V

Took her out into the gloamin'
Walked her right up to her door,
Told her t'was indeed a pleasure
Kissed her once but nothing' more

VI

Asked if I would come and see her,
Said her life was such a bore,
She would meet me on the corner
By the iron monger's store.

VII

So I promised, faithfully promised
Thought she was good company
Little guessed the wench was playin'
Wickedness I couldn't see

VIII

Met her on the walk at seven,
She was there as big could be
Promptly grasped me by an elbow
So the whole derned town could see.

IX

It was such a lovely movie,
Took her home right to her door,
Told her 'twas indeed a pleasure,
Kissed her twice but nothin' more.

X

Time went on, the plot grew thicker,
Romance blossomed in my breast
Couldn't pass those sacred portals
Though I tried my very best.

XI
Then one night the maiden weakened,
Led me in right through the hall,
Took me to her little parlor,
Seemed at last she'd heard loves call

XII
Hung my coat upon a hanger,
Locked the door and kept the key,
Pulled the blind down at the window
So her neighbors wouldn't see.

XIII
Sat us down upon the sofa,
Two soft arms 'bout me entwined
Woe oh woe poor Peter Milan
With a wife of this foul kind.

XIV
Deep we were in happy caress,
Came a soft step on the walk,
Swiftly did the maiden drop me
Straightened up her ruffled frock.

XV
Time for chivalry was over
Grabbed my coat in one swift sweep,
Toss'd the damsel in a corner.
Never let a single peep.

XVI
Crossed me quickly to the window,
Slipped it up and madly ran
Wasn't time to be a hero,,
'Twas no place to meet her man.

XVII
Doubled up the slippy sidewalk,
Heard a short and final bang,
Just another busted romance,
Hope the sucker doesn't hang.

XVIII
In the paper, "Sunday Mirror"
Scandal sheet most limeys buy,
Were a few short damning phrases,
Peter Milan doomed to die

XIX
Then my orders came for sailin'
Sailin' home across the sea,
But that restless spirit haunts me
Never more will I be free.

LESSON FOR OLD AGE DODGERS

When you're old and not contented
And beginning to resent it
Then its time to take a gander at yourself
Take a good look in a mirror
And thank God with holy fervor
That your state on earth is man, not mouse.

When you gaze upon the wrinkles
Just remember life is fickle
When you've reached the top its apt to let you down.
And when hair has turned to gray
Don't consider it that way
Just regard it as well deserved crown.

So pull up those aged pants
Give old ways a different slant
Take a lesson from the youngsters in the crowd
If it doesn't break your heart
All the folks will think you smart
And the world will sing your praises right out loud.

LATE SPRING

The ice was late in going out this year.
For days, the lake
In solemn spectral black
Lay motionless and still –
The sun rose cold,
Passed cold across the sky
And coldly set.
No robin came
to warm our winter hearts
With his bright song.
The marsh stood bleak and silent,
And little patches
Of coarse snow
Defaced the northern slope
Of each brown hill.

And then
One day at dawn
I heard the "caw"
Of nature's messenger,
And knew at once
Spring-time
Was on her way.

First Flight

The dawn breaks grey.
The wind is cold.
Across the steaming marshes
Little cat's-paws of fog rise up.
Men huddle in reed blinds
And murmur of past hunts.

A few yards out – dim silhouettes –
The decoys bob and weave
In tireless circling agitation;
The Judas of their kind.

With growing whisper
Out of deep lowering skies
Comes faint the whisper of a thousand wings.
The decoys pause in hushed expectancy.

With grating overtones
Of artificial man-made things
The deep quack quacking
Of a duck at feed
Rides loud and clear the wind.

From high above
On swooshing crescent wings
Thin triangles dip down at undetermined speeds.
Bluebills flash overhead.

In rapid fire staccato
Hot guns boom out
Grim messages of Death.
Soft bodies strew dark waters.
White streaks show swimming dogs
Whose barks ring through the marsh.

Slowly men stretch cramped limbs.
The smell of bottled coffee fills the air.
Outboards whine into life.
The morning flight is done.

STORM

Out of the shuddering night
Storm clouds came sweeping,
Lashing the laboring trees,
Driving them to their knees,
Heavy clouds weeping
Wild waves a-leaping.

Skies torn asunder.
Roarings of thunder
Lightning's fantastic glow
Casting on us below
Visions of Hellsfire
Breath of disaster.

"O race of evil men
Mark well our power
You have your fleeting day
We of all things may stay.
Voice of the thunder,
Flash of the lightning,
We are Imperishable.
We are Forever."

JUNE RAIN

The softest caress I know
Is the touch of rain
Cool and clear
Fondling my face with faint aroma
Of flower of locus.

The whispering of light winds
Through damp leaves –
The spongy feel of woodland sod
Under my feet
Fill me with unutterable delight.

The little bird upon the rain bejeweled branch
Sings with an utter abandon
As though his heart would break,
And my heart, like the bird's
Refreshed and cleansed from all its winter cares
Sings too.

Warnings

The foaming torrent of the years roll on.
Voice of Flood
Thunder on Thunder
Waters of a Man's life, hurriedly

Reflection of face, Nature's mirror
The shadowy Depths of Uncertain Existence
Fear and Hate,
Lust for gain.

A Raven croaks hoarse.
Over uncertain horizons
The Icons matter
Change Genes unaccountable.
Out of joint is our time.

Grim warnings confront us.
The Stone that shall shatter
Shall swirl, break the Pattern
Is Ours for the dropping.
Vain Creature this Man
To play God the Creator.

Encounter

Margy
Just one of those gals
Who leave you in need of a drink,
I think.

She's everyone's pal,
A wild sort of frivolous jade,
I'm afraid.

A wicked young maid,
The kind that you love and you leave,
I believe.

A bit of a flirt,
She winks as she sways gracefully by,
GUESS I'LL TRY.

ACADIA

(for Queen's University opera *Evangeline c1949*)

Acadia, homeland of our fathers,
Loud may our voices ring out in your praise
Dear to our hearts are in the murmuring forests
Your long rolling fields, where the sleek cattle graze.
Softly the wind blows in from the ocean
Carrying far inland the scent of the seas,
Pledging the land its lasting devotion,
Whispering its love on the wings of the breeze.

Acadia, homeland of our fathers,
Loud may our voices ring out in your praise.
Dear to our hearts are the hills and the headlands
Bathed by the morn in a shimmering haze.
Brightly the sun shines down on Acadia,
Loud roars the voice of the rivers and streams.
Gay are the hearts of Acadia's people,
Free as the fancies that pass in a dream.

QUITTING TIME

It's a very saddening sound to hear
The barman chant, "There's no more beer".
Upon his face a contented smirk
Glad to be finished the evening's work.
The noisy customers in the room
Hearing these words of impending doom
With disappointment upon each face
Staggering slightly leave the place,
Climb into autos as best they can.
God help the poor pedestrian.
The glasses which but an hour before
Had spattered foam on the barroom floor
Endearing each heart with a simple cheer
And the air with rich aroma of beer
Ranged in neat tiers the bars bare space
Cold, dry and clean in their rightful place.
The waiters, relieved of their bibs, once white
But soiled with the stains of a busy night
Roll down their sleeves, put the place in shape
And guzzle a pint for old time's sake.
Then leaving the comforting heat of the fire
Wend their way homeward, undress and retire.

THE HUNT

The mystique of the hunt!
Wild dreams of giant bucks
Gliding down narrow, dusky trails
In early morning light
Like grey ghosts of the dawn.

The raucous sound or irritated jay
Disturbed from early morning snooze –
A mallards loud "quack, quacking" from the bay –
And whirrings of a startled partridge wings
Imagining an enemy's approach.
Slowly the sun arises in the east,
For moments every single blade of grass
Dew laden sparkles in the light.
And with new dawn spawned breeze
A crimson leaf floats fluttering, spinning from above.

"Frozen", I sit in my orange splendour on a rise;
A doe, not much above a yearling size,
Sharp ears alert, moves by
Trailed by a dappled fawn.
She stops, they nose each other gently –
And are gone.
A chickadee parks on a limb nearby –
And piliated woodpecker
Sits dark against a shimmering birch.
Nature's awake!

There'll be no kill today.

Last Hunt

Weather turned cold last night!
Leaves once were soundless soft;
Cracked at every step
Until I reached my "stand".
Five hundred rafting ducks
In nearby bay
Lifted, and dived, and fluttered a thousand wings,
Quack, Quacking softly
In the freshening of the dawn!
And blue jays.
Sensing, perhaps a deer,
Began to call
Down by the gravel pit.
Off towards Benson,
Just as the sun broke forth,
A hound bayed,
Hot on the trail –
And I sat shivering
In my bright orange suit,
A startling contrast
To the shadows on the hill!
Impatiently, I listen for a shot
From Dave,
Scouring his land
Just one mile to the west.
But no shot comes!
The wind is cold.

Long fingers from the slowly rising sun
Throw blinding shafts of light
Over the trail I watch
For re-emergence of two
Small, cautious, does
That eyed me so intensely
Just last night.
Once more, I wait in vain!
No hesitating crunch of sharpened hooves
On frost filled leaves
Comes to my straining ears –
Suddenly,
The thought of toast, hot coffee
And real warmth
In nearby friendly kitchen
Arouses my old bones, and
Starts me, quick marching
Towards home.

Perhaps to-night – or never??
C'est la vie!

THE BALLAD OF SENATOR BILL

We've paddled the placid waters
Of the old Rideau Canal
From Crane's Nest to Burrett's Rapids
And our trips are always swell.
There were Bill and Ev and Jack and Gwen
And waters bright and clear
With Mary and I in our freight canoe
Always bringing up the rear.
And Bill and Ev in their Kevlar dream
Well out in front of the pack
'Twas a wonder to see Bill glide through the trees
His canoe upon his back

We'd travelled one day from a little isle
In the centre of Big Mud lake,
And tired and sore returned to shore
Where the Rideau waters break
At the Narrows Lock, a tiny stop
On the Rideau's great divide.
And we'd asked the friendly lockmaster
For a placed where we could 'bide.

We had pitched our tent well above the lock
In a little clearing there
Surrounded by lilac bushes
Where the breeze was fresh and fair
With tents erected and ready,

And cooking fires alight
We'd decided to have a couple of drinks
To start the evening right.

Across the road was a government house
And the "can" was far away,
Especially for six grey travelers
Who'd sat in canoes all day.
And Jack had a fussy bladder
'Twas a hard one to control
And it boded no hesitation
Nor a long and dusty stroll.
When the urge to go came to him
He just simply had to stop,
And head for the nearest bushes
Whether they were high or not.

So on that fateful evening
The expected came to pass,
But Jack little knew that across the road
There dwelled a curious lass,
The friend of the "Southern Manager"
Who had little else to do
But sit with a pair of "glasses"
And scan the evening view.

Unaware of impending disaster
We went about out chores
Until 10 o'clock when we felt the urge
to find the washroom doors.

Now Mary and Ev and Gwendolyn
Were always slow in the spot;
And we three stalwart gentlemen
Were a speedy, speedy lot.

So it happened we were waiting
Outside the women's door
When wild Mel Tell the manager
Approached us with a roar
And for the next few minutes
Condemned us far and wide
For Jack's wee indiscretion
Observed by Mel Tell's bride.

He threatened us with consequence
Too terrible to explore,
And left us pale and shaking
Outside the washroom door.

However, the next morning,
Still stinging from our fright
We quickly devised a little scheme
To set the matter right.
And Jack became "the General"
And Bill, "The Senator",
And I was given the dirty job
Of evening up the score.

Now Gord that wise old lockmaster
And well beknown to us
Apologized that morning for his miserable boss
So then I quickly answered
In tones quiet and sincere
To thank Gordon for his trouble
And said to have no fear.
For the General wasn't angry;
He met asses every day
But the Senator was roaring mad
What he'd do, I couldn't say
But I thought a serious reprimand

Would go to old Mel Tell,
And it might be, that one short pee
Could blow his job to hell.

And I knew as soon as I said it,
By the look on Gordon's face
That the manager would shortly know
Of his threatened fall from grace.

And it came to pass, that that silly ass
Just lasted out the year
And was then retired from the Rideau Canal
Just as we'd led him to fear.
Now up and down the waterway
The rumour was soon afloat
That Tell had insulted a Senator
Who'd locked through in his boat –
And the Senator had reported him
To his high political friends
And that old Mel Tell for his hasty tongue
Had to come to a fitting end.

Then someone leaked the true tale
Of how the deed was done;
And laughter rolled down the Rideau Canal
In the brilliant summer sun.

So "Senator Bill" still drives his canoe
Wherever the hell he likes
And "General Jack" still has his pee
Wherever the spirit strikes.
And Ev and Gwen and Mary
Chatter quietly from above
As we paddle the placid waters
Of that beautiful canal.

OLD AGE

They sit there
Stuffing intently
Multi-colored pills
In little boxes –
Carefully marked
For each day of the week.
With wrinkled hands
And thickened, blackened nails
And tiny purple blotches
On ancient withering skin,
They sit.
Blear-eyed
They face the struggles of the day:
The times for pills
On which their lives depend.
So it would seem.
And will the Children call???
The meals become
The one bright light
That marks their darkening hours –
A slice of toast, a cup of tea, a lettuce sandwich-
But then,
A supper out!

Aches plague the failing bones
"There's two of us –
That's all that's left,"

Repeats itself incessantly –
As stories oft repeated
Now repeats.
And conversations
Centre on the dying and the dead –
On grandchildren
Now grown and in the world!
The latest antics
Of the T.V. clown –
And how the breakfast egg was underdone!
At last comes sleep –
And they are young again.

Woman of War

She stands there, wispy broom in work worn hand
The living symbol of a war torn land.
With dead impassive eye, she views the throng.
The Khaki columns as they plod along
The smell of death hangs in the morning air
She doesn't seem to know, or doesn't care
Within the battered soil her husband sleeps
She lifts her broom, and slowly starts to sweep.

GLOSSARY

William Acton — campers at Chaffey's for many years – Mr. Acton Sr. had curious pets – (snakes and skunks). He was long time owner of property on which Queen's University built its Biological Station. Bill, his son, paratrooper in U.S. and served in the Aleutian Islands, Italy and France – the third-fourth generations of this family still return to Chaffeys for holidays and one, Chuck and his wife Trish and their daughter have recently started to make Chaffey's their home.

Busty & Ted Ashbaugh — Used to tent on Boathouse Point near the Locks – from Youngstown, Ohio – Came to Canada and Chaffey's prior to 1920 – Busty was a physical education teacher in the States – two children, Pete and Teddy who came back for a number o years – great friends of the Warrens.

Frank Best — once cheese maker in Opinicon Village – later moved to Chaffey's into house transported down the lake, to near the lock. Owner and operator of the machine to saw wood in the spring – always enjoyed "snuff" – extremely likeable – Ross, one of his younger sons, retired at Chaffey's

Tim Bevens   professional guide and hunter – lived at Chaffey's for many years as a fishing guide – became my image of a great hunter and fisherman – caught, with client, an over 35 pound salmon with a permanent customer, D. F. Anderson from Youngstown, Ohio, circa 1937

Mr. Cordes   camper on Boathouse Point at Chaffey's very British from Civil Service in Ottawa.

Tom & Francis Davis   (nee: Regan). Long time Chaffey's residents – Tom for many years a Captain on the Great Lakes – known to have hired many local young men for his crew. Affectionately referred to by some of his sailors as "Roaring Tom". Many good stories of sailing in Gulf of St. Lawrence during WWII – large family. Francis ran summer cottages at Chaffey's for many years, daughter Mary and her husband Bill Hamilton took over cottages after they retired – other family members scattered.

John Dorey   an elderly, well respected guide, known partially for his love of Euchre – a very fine fishing guide.

"Clinter" Fleming   A descendant of the first Lockmaster at Chaffey's – exceptional guide – in association with an American tourist, wrote a semi-imaginary book on fishing in the Chaffey's area called "When the Fish are Rising" now out of print for some years.

George Franklin originally worked in a sawmill on Opinicon Lake – later, became a permanent guide from Simmon's Resort, chewed plug tobacco like my father – while guiding from Simmon's Resort worked for Peter Hayden who was one of Chaffey's first U.S. fishermen – he and George given credit for setting up many bass shelters in Opinicon Lake.

Helen Gourley my teacher for at least three or four years at Pine Grove – one of the best teachers I ever knew. She was quite adept with a strap.

Bill Gifford son of George Gifford who was Chaffey's Station master – Bill died young.

Buenavista one of the last cargo ships to use the Rideau System – very resounding whistle – scared horses to death.

Don & Hazel Jarrett operated the Opinicon Hotel – originally from the U.S. and at that time clientele mostly U.S. citizens – very interested in the community – had pictures of all activities in the 1930's and earlier. Don, a very talented man. Hazel also a citizen of U.S. Great organizer and supporter of the Chaffey's Lock Women's' Institute – particularly visible in spotting alcohol in the hall at dances.

Richard Mahoney	longtime resident and outstanding fishing guide at Chaffey's Lock. He was married to Pearl Doyle and they had two daughters, Eleanor (an artist) and Marion, now retired – "Dick" fished with one U.S. family for many years – one of the early "tree fishers" – could have been anything he wanted had he lived in today's society. He and my father used to help pack the ice when it was brought to the ice houses in the winter.
Bob Lasha	a well known fishing guide in the 1920s and 30s – a short man who operated a St. Lawrence Skiff – he was particularly helpful to amateurs, such as I was, and taught us a good deal about the channels which were open before the Locks were built – he was an expert at his trade.
Dugal MacIntyre	Scots – lived in Ottawa – later built a house in Chaffey's and retired there – worked for many years with Ottawa Water and Electric – guided some after retirement – one son – Doug – worked for Bell Telephone and eventually retired here.
Professor Lisse	Mary Lou and Marion – daughters of a professor from State College – extra fine voices and led singing at campfires on the Point.
Cliff & Ella Pennock	my landlord when I was in school in Elgin – no children so kept four or five of us in Bank and School – Cliff best pictures

available of life at the Opinicon where he cut hair – were like a father and mother to me during the weeks at school.

Allie Patterson operated two large cars to carry young people who wanted to go to Athens for Grade 13 in late 30s , also operator of what then a private telephone service – hot tempered but well liked and respected – eventually owned a large school bus service to Athens and some rural schools.

Cook Rowswell families came to the area from Somerset, England before the Canal was built c1818. Cook was a farmer when I first met him who sold frogs to fishermen at the Lock – descendants related to us through our grandmother, Ellen Rowswell.

Ned Rowswell lockman at Chaffey's circa 1920s – brother of Ellen Rowswell, our grandmother – in this area before Chaffey built his mill – said to have been related to the Poole girl who married Sam Chaffey – my father called him Uncle Ned

Rowswell's Creek in 1860s sported a mill near north end of what is now known as Murphy's Bay – excellent clear stream in my school days at Pine Grove – pike came up creek to spawn as did suckers – now clogged by beaver dams and is very silted – fish now unable to come up from Opinicon Lake.

Simmon's Farm now belongs to Jamie Simmons (the 5th I

believe) – originally used as a farm – later became a fishing lodge – still operating as a fishing lodge in the summer – use to be a number of guides operating through there – grandfather a real politician – poem called "Simmon's Bull" still in existence with "Pep" Burt.

Sawyers	with Frank Best, men who assisted in the cutting of firewood into 16" stove lengths
Mattie Stanton	a student who travelled to Athens for Grade 13 with Allie Patterson's busses – often teased – very good-natured.
Lindsay Smith	a very good pal of mine at Athens H.S. great daredevil – according to reports, killed in WWII – a sad loss to society.
Henry Smith	a well respected fishing guide into the 1950s – had very loyal clients who came back year after year to the Opinicon – large family from Elgin area – family still in vicinity.
Virr Family	believe of English descent – from Civil Service in Ottawa – one son a graduate from RMC – shuttled planes to Europe during the war – his brother, Bob, also involved as a flier during WWII – spent many summers on Mill Point at Chaffey's.
Jack & Ellen Warren	(nee Rowswell) – Jack, son of Noel Warren, born at Chaffey's Lock circa 1852 near what is now Wild Apple Hill development – married

Ellen Rowswell, a girl living in Clear Lake area – children, Mame, Will, Herm, Dinah, Emma – Ellen's ancestors came from Somerset England – had settled in Clear Lake area – Herm served with P.P.C.L.I. in Battle of Cambrai and was badly wounded – job after war on lock at Newboro – later Lockmaster at Chaffey's until 1956– 57. Herm's wife Alice Thompson was from near Burridge – her mother was a Barr – she was very interested in sending we kids to school – and did – she was a strong feminist and generally controlled the thinking at home – a wonderful cook – wouldn't eat fish. Admired her father, an Irish policeman, a great deal.

Henry White

a well known farmer and guide in the 1930s – somewhat eccentric, fond of cars which were scarce and expensive in those days – sometimes teased by his fishing clients – seemed to have bad feelings toward lock keepers – who, in self defense, didn't like him.

Women's Institute

a powerful organization in the 1930s, 40s and 50s – nearly all community women members and organization popular throughout Canada – money made for operation by dances, turkey dinners etc. – dances usually supervised by Frances Davis, Jenny Laishley, Alice Warren, Mrs. Wiltshire, Hazel Jarrett and others from time to time – kept order – no drinking booze – offenders often thrown out and

not allowed back in – really tough crowd!
Repeat offenders now and then cooled off
by dumping in canal.

www.ingramcontent.com/pod-product-compliance
Lightning Source LLC
Chambersburg PA
CBHW030927090426
42737CB00007B/343